Integrative
Group
Therapy

Integrative Group Therapy

The Structured Five-Stage Approach

Second Edition

MILDRED ROSS, MS, OTR

SLACK Incorporated, 6900 Grove Road, Thorofare, New Jersey, 08086

SLACK International Book Distributors

In Canada:
  McGraw-Hill Ryerson Limited
  300 Water Street
  Whitby, Ontario
  L1N 9B6

In Europe and the United Kingdom:
  Quest-Meridien Ltd.
  145a Croydon Road
  Beckenham, Kent BR3 3RB
  England

In Australia and New Zealand:
  MacLennan & Petty Pty Limited
  P.O. Box 425
  Artarmon, N.S.W. 2064
  Australia

In Japan:
  Igaku-Shoin, Ltd.
  Tokyo International P.O. Box 5063
  1-28-36 Hongo, Bunkyo-Ku
  Tokyo 113
  Japan

In Asia and India:
  PG Publishing Pte Limited.
  36 West Coast Road, #02-02
  Singapore 0512

Foreign Translation Agent

  John Scott & Company
  International Publishers' Agency
  417-A Pickering Road
  Phoenixville, PA 19460
  Fax: 215-988-0185

Executive Editor: Cheryl D. Willoughby
Publisher: Harry C. Benson

Printed in the United States of America

Library of Congress Catalog Card Number: 88-043457

ISBN 1-55642-083-8

Published by: SLACK Incorporated
              6900 Grove Road
              Thorofare, NJ 08086-9447

Last digit is print number: 10   9   8   7   6   5   4   3   2   1

CONTENTS

PREFACE

More than 10 years have passed since the introduction of the Five-Stage group approach for populations in long-term care. This book reflects the experience and knowledge gained since that time. Intended to be a flexible framework, the Five-Stages demonstrated that updated theories, emerging treatment techniques, and new modalities can be incorporated into the Five-Stages. This book preserves the Five-Stages, but offers a new and clarifying look at underlying premises for treatment approach and selection of activities. As a basic structure, the Five-Stages require knowledge from many resources to allow it to have meaning for therapists and members alike. It is difficult to achieve a productive, satisfying encounter with non-responsive group members in special populations. A consistent and productive group requires ever-increasing knowledge of new concepts and a willingness to study resources for theories and application. Susan Fine, MA, OTR, FAOTA, observed that,

> "it is often necessary to combine several schools of thought and draw from many resources when working with populations whose illness reflect biopsychosocial phenomena. Neither the patient, or the course of a given illness, are unidimensional. Different treatment models can augment or jointly stimulate desired effects; and changing needs certainly may require different approaches" (Fine, 1989).

In my opinion, this can be applied to all populations addressed by this book.

Also, cognizance is taken of the great diversities and complexities of these populations. Therefore, the chapter on "Relevance of Sensory Integration and Other Theoretical Treatment Approaches to the Five-Stage Group" was written to underscore and address the origins of skill and how it may be achieved.

The Five-Stage is a comprehensive approach for presenting selected sensory stimuli in an organized, systemic manner. It provides a structure for the most effective and consistent results with populations *where making contact is difficult and the usual group approach does not work.* A number of group approaches for chronic populations have been published. The Five-Stage concept can be the method of choice when treating the moderately to severely neurologically impaired adult, young or old.

There are special reasons for each stage and these must be understood. Understanding the format will enhance and may be used with groups the therapist conducts, such as living skills groups, exercise, craft, and current events groups. How do we convey welcome, create alertness, present the task for acceptance and satisfaction or the task that will motivate and contribute cumulatively to cognitive responses? In the Five-Stages, it is the sequential way in which selected activities are introduced in a group format and how they are presented that can help to prepare the central nervous system to integrate the sensory information for an adaptive response. Therapists can recognize their own immediate success and research can establish longer lasting effectiveness. *Welcome to the Five-Stage Group!*

ACKNOWLEDGEMENTS

Acknowledgements to the First Edition

This manual started out as four pages that would help staff survive where few wished to serve. In this respect, it is a beginner's manual. The fact that this manual has been organized and published is due to the encouragement of Brenda Smaga, MS, OTR, Director of Rehabilitation Services at Connecticut Valley Hospital. She took time to read the contents and to contribute valuable criticisms, thoughts, and relevant material. Ms. Smaga has a quick comprehension and the ability to empower.

Josephine C. Moore, PhD, OTR, FAOTA, has been kind enough to correspond actively with us on the clarification of the rationale underlying the descriptions of the five stages of the group, as well as review statements referring to neurophysiology. Dr. Moore is a Professor in the Department of Anatomy, University of South Dakota Medical School. While taking full responsibility for interpretation of her explanations, we are grateful and proud to have her permission to acknowledge her valuable assistance and encouragement.

The format and activities described in this manual have been generated by the creative, courageous, and innovative treatment approach for psychiatric patients proposed by Lorna Jean King, OTR, FAOTA, and Leona Richman, OTR. Also, we recognize the powerful influence of A. Jean Ayers, PhD, OTR, FAOTA, in the application of her theory for use in treatment.

When the Sensory-Motor-Cognitive Test in this manual was originally published many letters were received requesting the Lela Llorens test. Permission has been obtained from Ms. Llorens, OTR, FAOTA, to include her test in the assessment. We have great admiration for her comprehensive organization of the whole area of testing, evaluation, recommendations, and treatment goals for the patient. These provide a valuable learning experience from which we could draw. Ms. Llorens' test is administered quickly, does not require much explanation for the aphasic patient, offers a quick appraisal of a patient's attitude in approaching a task, and demonstrates his degree of organization. Valnere McLean, OTR, FAOTA, contributed her thoughts and suggestions to the material we have added to the second printing. Her sensitivity, knowledge, and sincerity have promoted our professional growth.

We are in the debt of Arnold Eastman, who used his audiovisual skills to enhance and facilitate learning and therapy. The following outstanding individuals have helped us with their capable skills: Marion Harris, Secretary of Rehabilitation Services; Celia Yarbrough, RN; and Mary Hickey, Psychiatric Aide. Appreciation is expressed to the following doctors with whom dialogue has been so helpful. Benjamin Macdonald, MD; Francisco Quintana, MD, Unit Chief, Geriatric Service of Connecticut Valley Hospital; and Karoline Ascher, MD, Chief of the Chronic Disability Program, Cedarcrest Hospital, Newington.

Finally, the unique contribution our families have provided must be fully acknowledged. To Roger Burdick and Sara-Ann Ross, special mention is made with regard to their illustrations.

—Mildred Ross, OTR
Assistant Unit Chief, Geriatric Services
—Dona Burdick, MS
Recreation Therapist
Connecticut Valley Hospital
Middletown, Connecticut

Acknowledgements to the 2nd Edition

Time has changed the locations of most of the persons referred to above, but not the deep appreciation that I feel as many continue to provide me with their support and wisdom. In addition, gratitude is extended also to Marli Cole-Schiraldi, OTR, for her enlightenment on research relating to the SARIB Assessment; to Beth Fisher, BS, Mental Health Case Manager; Toby Goldschneider, COTA; Carole Kerkin, MS, Director of Human Services of Goodwill Industries; and Barbara Panzer, OTR, for their very valuable and collaborative assistance in reading portions of the manuscript relating to the validation of the conduct of specific groups; to John Murray, Media Specialist, Manchester Community College, for his photography and patience;, and to Sharon Lajoie, RTD and Janet Gregor, OTR, for providing tremendous support. A very special thanks goes to the Hebrew Home and Hospital of Hartford, Connecticut, and, in particular, to Joan Grey, RPT, Director of Rehabilitation, for making this site available for testing.

Mildred Ross, OTR/L
Private Practice, New Britain, Connecticut

INTRODUCTION

Except for individual differences that make each of us unique, the same centers and nerve pathways serve similar functions for both the child and the adult of any age. The same principles of neurophysiology are applicable and adaptable to all age groups. It is these principles of how the nerve system functions that underlie the activities described in this manual. That is why the presentation, sequence, and selection of stimuli for the Five-Stage are based upon what is understood from neurophysiological principles taken from treatment approaches used with children or adults.

The following assumptions are made:

1. Stimulation/activities have properties that affect the central nervous system (CNS).
2. Not only selected vestibular, tactile, or other sensory stimuli promote the brain's ability to register, organize, and respond adaptively, but also an organized sequence of inputs enhances the response and response probability.
3. That response to stimulation/activity by individuals in special populations only can be motivated, heightened, and possibly only improved by activities that are being presented in a sequential, systematic way.
4. A routine of organized sequences restores the likelihood of an automatic habitual response.
5. When neurologically impaired individuals register the sights, sounds, touch, and tastes in their environment and find it pleasurable, they are motivated to interact and habituate the experience.

6. An aversive stimulus also engages the CNS and organizes a protective response to it. This response may be fear or heightened alertness and may result in angry outbursts (fight) or withdrawl (flight).
7. Aspects of both kinds of stimuli are to be used knowledgeably so as to motivate individuals to interact with their environment.
8. Neurologically impaired individuals appear to only marginally interact with their environment.
9. The Five-Stage Group appears to restore environmental interaction.

Smelling baking bread, stroking a soft furry animal, eating creamy ice cream, or getting a hug usually can make us feel good, help us to attend to the task and to sustain response. The opposite condition also exists. An unknown noise, a disheartening admonition, an ice cube down the back, or the odor of a skunk usually can make us attend but may repel, inhibit, or disorganize a response. How to use some of both aspects advantageously is the task of this book to demonstrate.

Special populations are those groups of individuals who require more than the usual amount of cues and assists for their CNS to become organized sufficiently to make an appropriate and sustained response. Their nervous systems require assistance from the environment and their caregivers to perform adaptively. The Five-Stages provide the structure and routine for groups to offer the unusual degree and strength of cues and assists that will prod the nervous system to organize a meaningful response. The course of the stages appears to help assimilation of the sensory inputs and to aid organization for a motor output or response. An example of this is seen in the reflective research of Corcoran, 1987.

All Five-Stages should be accomplished in each session so that the accumulative effect will help achieve goals. Each stage is described in detail and suggested activities are provided. More activities and explanations of neurophysiological principles involved are addressed in Ross, 1987. However, the emphasis is not on *what* shall we do in group today, but on *how* shall we present movement, a perceptual task, or a thoughtful exercise, and *when* is that activity appropriate so that an organized response may result.

Therapists trained in the use of activity and activity analysis have a unique approach to groups with special populations. Goals, methods, activity analysis, and response to group dynamics within a group session are unique and require additional consideration from what is generally taught about groups (Ross, 1987). Understanding the roles of group members and group development is not applicable as is taught, in the traditional sense, to groups where the action is emphasized as the response and language is not the main means of expressing the learning that may take place. The groups here are social and task oriented. The outcome expected is environmental interaction, movement, and cognitive response.

Three criteria are used to evaluate the benefit of each session.

1. Each group member will demonstrate acceptable behavior during the session.
2. Each participant will participate in at least one activity.
3. At the end of the session, the prevailing mood should be an alert calmness.

The Five-Stages of a Group comprise:

Stage I: This stage uses as many of the senses as is possible and reasonable to arouse and to welcome group members, as well as to promote some continuity with the previous group meeting. This stimulation signals the reticular activating and limbic system of the central nervous system that something interesting, physically comfortable, and emotionally safe is present. This stage promotes sensory registration.

Stage II: This stage uses activity that emphasizes movement or bodily responses. Gross and proximal movement patterns are used to facilitate muscle tone, postural alignment, and body awareness and scheme. The stimulation to the central nervous system is provided by proprioceptive, kinesthetic, tactile, vestibular, auditory, and visual inputs. The cerebellum, brain stem, thalamus, widespread cortical areas, and basal ganglia are some of the important structures that are influenced. This stage promotes sensory stimulation and integration.

Stage III: This stage uses activities that will offer the opportunity for sensory information to be modified and made meaningful as an adaptive response. The brain stem, thalamus, and the cortex are stimulated in this way. This stage promotes the display of sensory integration.

Stage IV: This stage uses activities that facilitate organized thought and behavior to be demonstrated in action, verbalizations, and inter-relatedness. Cortical integration is affected.

Stage V: This stage employs familiar activities that signal closing of the session on a positive, affirmative note. This provides another opportunity to generate the natural responses to pleasure and the reinforcement of internal control (Ross, 1987, pg. 82) as appropriate leavetaking, handclasps, reminders, and promises are offered. Stimulation is directed to the reticular formation and limbic systems to preserve an emotional tone of calm alertness. This stage engenders environmental trust.

The therapist is an interactive facilitator and part of the environment who must move about, provide appropriate touching, use a calm voice and make eye contact to obtain membership involvement. Members may reject involvement for a while, differ in their individual requirement of physical contact, or designate other kinds of contact. These conditions must be respected. More study, research, and personal observations will help us progress to greater understanding of subtle cues in each individual.

The therapist arrives with a plan. Feelings and needs exist within the group that may be at variance with the plan, and in any stage the plan may be redirected by the group members as they have things to teach us, too. *Always observe response and be guided by it in modifying your input.* The whole person is involved in all the stages, as is his total nervous system. The Five-Stages require a high level of therapeutic judgment to juggle neurofacilitation techniques, environmental realities, equipment, and the dynamics of group process all at once; but the challenge remains irresistible and satisfying.

For purposes of convenience, in this book, the group member is referred to as "he" and therapist as "she."

CHAPTER 1

Stage I
Beginning the Group
Session With An Orientation

In the first stage, three specific areas are of concern to the therapist so that the best possible beginning may be achieved for the group. First, each participant is acknowledged and welcomed individually. Second, the purpose of the group is stated briefly. Third, the awareness and attention of each member are obtained as much as it is likely to happen. The therapist should promptly move on to the next stage as soon as these goals are achieved, which is the extent the therapist considers to be the group's capacity for arousal. Accomplishing all five stages is required for the full benefits of a group. Pacing and timing when to move on, as the goals of each stage are achieved, are crucial.

Special populations need a special emphasis in the area of welcome that must never be overlooked. The special emphasis is on helping members to feel wanted, safe, and expectant with abundant assurances. The therapist signals this when she arranges a comfortable seating plan for each member, in a clean space, with pleasant sounds, and she wears a glad smile. When she touches appropriately as she greets participant personally, and finds some little surprise to distribute, she reassures everyone nonverbally that this is where everyone wants to be. Additional ideas for this, as well as suggestions for interesting items or ways for arousing attentiveness, are described below.

A reminder of the purpose of the group can be provided with a brief description. Examples are: "We meet here to do some work together and to share our thoughts, which can be helpful to all of us"; "We meet to exercise, to learn some new activity, and to talk together, or simply," "We meet to feel better." The group that meets regularly eventually may be ready to state its own purpose or describe what occurs during a session.

This structured beginning can be as brief as 5 minutes or about a fifth of the allotted time for the group session. The group may present with chaos, apathy, or unrelatedness, and these feelings must be dissipated before group members can begin to focus and sustain the needed interest to continue participation. A course is being set by which we can achieve more organized, meaningful, and satisfying thought and behavior. Individual problems and conversations are encouraged to wait until Stage IV so as not to divert the group away from the course of this process. A sincere promise to reopen or continue the conversation or problem "after we finish some work" is acceptable. By Stage IV, usually the conversation can include everyone and the problems appear to resolve themselves more easily through the very process in which the group members have been involved.

This initial stage of the group session is to be used to arouse the alerting and pleasure centers of the participants. A variety of activities that offer 30 seconds to 1 minute of handling and mastery are suggested. More specifically:

1) Introductions: Including the therapist, each group member states his name. Everyone can hold hands. Members can take turns ringing a bell or using a variety of bells, eg, there are heavy and light bells, miniature gongs, and bells that require palm pressure. Other musical instruments, such as cymbals, instruments to strum or pick, or an accordion for eliciting high or low notes can be explored enjoyably by group members. Above, we mentioned a little surprise that can be passed around and introducing an unexpected item can be that surprise.

   "Hello" can be said in a foreign language, by using sign language, or in a whisper. Whispering can effectively subdue a young, boisterous group. The handclasp and introduction can be provided individually by therapist or another member of the group who will volunteer. There are a variety of ways for touching when greeting. Some like touching palms as in the "patty cake" or another position. Saying "hello" or other greeting two or three times serves to reinforce each member's awareness and his presence.

2) Some ways of touching can be to offer a quick stretch to extensors by a moderate push on both shoulders of each group member. Demonstrate this first on the co-therapist or on a patient to whom this is acceptable. Check briefly thereafter with each member for acceptability. This can be an enjoyable and calming sensory input.

3) Present vibrator. (See chapter 9.) Provide, additionally, slow vestibular

input to a distractible group by having members hold hands and move slowly in a circle. The therapist stands outside the circle and uses the vibrator on the backs of each member as they approach her.

4) To collect and sustain the interest of group members, pass an item around that forces continual interaction with others and centralizes action. Introduce these imaginatively. These may be:

a. Spiny, rough, or textured items that may be rubbed on arms or touched to face. Change to soft items like a fluffy powder puff.

b. Perfume or aftershave can be offered to be placed on the wrist of group members. This will be calming.

c. Use any game device to single out which two members should say hello to each other; for example, one member can toss out a 6-foot rope in the direction of another member and may then walk on top of it to that member to say "hello." Young adults enjoy this. Two members can meet hopping toward each other or other variation.

d. Some sugarless candy, cracker, or small piece of fruit or drink may be served to a volatile group to ease tensions and help them relax.

e. The therapist may stand in the center and throw a 1 lb weight bean bag to each member twice around to increase attention, especially when there is agitation or distractibility. Then members may be able to throw it among themselves. This leads nicely into the next stage where more movement can be programmed.

f. Some noise makers require a squeeze to produce a sharp sound. Pass the object around once then pass it around again requiring group members to use another means to make the noise, such as putting object between knees or under arms. These can be found in gift stores or party shops. Other types of noise makers can be used.

g. There are wands and objects like globes, that when turned or jostled present floating specks that cause members to focus. If it is a wand, it may be used in movement such as rolled to each other on the floor or each member can demonstrate its use in a special way they choose.

h. Many different varieties of music boxes exist that require pressure on a part or turning a knob for playing. Some just require lifting a lid. This can be reused in Stage IV or V for reinforcement as most group members enjoy music and respond well.

i. A heavy item such as a gong, stone, plant, bar bell, bean bag, paperweight, book, sculpture, picture, tray, or a heavy metal object are just some examples of weighted objects to use that have a calming effect. Discussion need not ensue as they can be introduced as an item therapist wishes to share. The therapist must assist and prevent mishandling.

j. Museums and fairs sell toys and appliances of yesteryear that are easy and fun to manipulate such as "Jacob's Ladder," the "Busy Wheel," and the "Indian Windmill" (World Wide Games). The windmill has a blade, similar to a plane's propeller, that turns right or left depending on how a rubbing stick moves across the notches on the handle. The busy wheel is a button spinning on strings pulled in and out using both hands in a coordinated manner. The therapist can use hands for guidance. Museums stores have items that, as they are handled, fall into different shapes or reconstruct themselves in different patterns. They are fascinating and provide a feeling of accomplishment when mastered. Some very low-functioning groups may manage them, whereas an intellectual group may find them too difficult.

k. Stroll a marionette around the group and have members try it.

l. Candle collections to pass around can offer a theme for the day's program as part of a religious, historical, or cultural event. Candles can be scented and come in a variety of shapes, weights, and textures so that many sensory centers are stimulated at once.

m. Different bars of soap can be passed around to smell, to identify shapes, or to feel how shapes conform to the hand; eg, a small rose shape is quite different from the square of "Ivory" or the curve of "Dove." The rough textured soap used in factories for cutting hand grease will give a different sensation. This activity can be used in Stages III or IV for longer discussions. Pass the soaps around again and ask, "Who has the largest, the smallest, the prettiest, the nicest color, the strongest smell?"

n. Pass around one, but not more than two, strong odors for a passive group. These may be, for example, an empty jar retaining the odor of vinegar, mustard, garlic or onion, or a cotton ball soaked with lemon or almond flavor. For an excited group, odors such as potpourri or vanilla can be beneficial for calming. Pass the same odor around two or three times. Invite some small interaction.

o. When the group must operate at a very slow pace and is unable to sustain holding hands, try for just holding a neighbor's hand with therapist monitoring and reinforcing. Follow up with the following two activities.

p. Any way of suggesting breathing, such as a deep breath, a big sigh, or holding up one's index finger and blowing on it to feel the breath, blowing out a candle or blowing on a feather are ways of inducing relaxation to promote participation. Pass around a pinwheel to blow; the most resistive patient will usually attempt this. Sometimes pinwheels have several little wheels that challenge members to blow hard enough to turn a number of the wheels at one time.

q. Pass along touch. Light touch is alerting, stimulating, and can be somewhat irritating. It may be used to elicit reaction that can be quickly diverted to an agreeable interest. A way to elicit this is to request that people tap, pat, or stroke some part of the face, such as their cheeks or chin. The therapist can demonstrate using tips of fingers, brushing face lightly (as if drawing a cat's whiskers). One group member can pat another on the shoulder or the knee to be passed along to another. If someone in the group does not want to pass it along, the therapist can substitute and perform this action for a willing member.

r. Using a 5-pound weight within a bright yellow oilcloth covering has been successful with all levels of developmental disabilities. It can be passed around from member to member at first, then balanced on the head, shoulder, or knee, and finally thrown to each other (See Chapter 8 for precautions). The "hoppity-hop" ball (Flaghouse) can be used in similar fashion with a younger population. First it can be passed with right hand only, then the left hand, then from one hand to another and passed along. It can be raised above the head, held by therapist for each member to punch, and finally thrown to each other. People feel good to perform with it and to watch others.

s. With a group that is familiar to therapist, initial interaction can be invited by therapist putting on a lei, taking it off and placing it over the head of the next person. Each group member gets a turn to do this with a lei, crown, or something appealing. The lei can be limp, so obtaining a firmer, similar item for some populations who have motor planning or other sensory problems is suggested.

t. Such items as a Chinese yo yo, a giant yo yo, or a 'slinky' can go around to be used individually by each member in turn.

5) A feeling can be written on colorful construction paper and passed around to each patient randomly. Each group member may accept the feeling on the paper they received or state that their feelings differ. Additional variations can be:

a. Present feeling words (ie, angry, pretty, grumpy, joyful) on cards cut in different shapes such as triangles, rectangles, octagons, etc. The therapist can talk about the shapes, ask participants to choose a feeling and, if they like, to use masking tape and attach it to themselves.

b. Present blank shapes and have group members write their own feelings on the shape. Give the members masking tape so they may put it on themselves wherever they choose.

c. Ask two or three group members, whom the therapist feels may be most receptive, to act out their feelings and then ask others to join them. The therapist models her feeling first. It is easy to model a feeling of relaxation, sleepiness, or happiness as examples. This can be a good prelude to movement. Feelings expressed are not for discussions that may become judgmental; rather they can be reintroduced in Stage IV as a means for discussing changes in feelings that may occur during the course of the group session.

6) Consider the relationship between the positioning arrangement of group members and the message this implies to each group member as the group session begins:

   a. Form a circle with members all standing. This may be the most desirable situation, but it requires group members who are in control, possess some endurance, and have a fair level of interest as well as a sense of conformity. It can be a working objective to bring group members to this level of functioning.

   b. Group members are seated in straight chairs in a circle. This is more relaxing and can prevent wandering as well as decrease inattentiveness. The proximity of each member to the others also can be noted as the group will indicate its wishes in a nonverbal manner. Sometimes knees can be touching and arms can go around the necks of neighbors; with other groups, this is not possible. Each group demonstrates its tolerance for degree of closeness and distancing.

   c. Varying the seating arrangements alone introduces a novelty into the group to which there will be changed responses. Seat group members around a table; arrange seating in two rows of chairs facing each other; or, arrange a circle of chairs, but instead of chairs facing the center, have two chairs face each other with two backs touching all around the circle, thus causing participants to turn to one side to see what is going on inside the circle while facing directly one other person.

   d. Sit on the floor. This can lower tensions and is not desirable for a sluggish group. Activities must be fast-paced to promote cohesiveness. This, sometimes, may be the best means to start off a boisterous group or to end an excited group as it offers a measure of organization and control.

   e. Use the hand rails along the wall of a facility for group members to hold on to for some support and conduct a group. This was successful with a geriatric group with psychiatric problems. Stage II then consisted of ballet movements, followed by returning to chairs for a Stage III activity.

7) To a new group with fair cognition, offer a basket filled with a variety of objects from which to choose. The ability to hold the basket and pick something out may not be possible but should be considered. Some members who appear to want to do so may tell why they chose the item. This can be appropriate for a group where there is some uncertainty as to what to expect as therapist has an opportunity to model safety, consideration, and support by not urging anyone to take an item or to talk about it.

8) Group members, after introductions, can write their names on an upright portable blackboard or large upright easel pad that can be brought to each member, or those who can may walk to the board. Very low functioning groups, who have retained ability to sign name, perform this willingly as it is a significant way to reinforce self-awareness.

One or two of the above suggestions may be used each time the group meets. Adding one different task that provides a quick mastery brings early assurance that one belongs here and will succeed. Each performance should be encouraged by an appropriate, positive, and sincere comment from therapist. The therapist initiates readiness to move on to Stage II.

Your Own Suggestions Below:

CHAPTER 2

Stage II
Movement Is Emphasized

In this stage, movement activities that alert and excite or calm and relax are offered according to need. It combines the use of objects to hold and use in movement with the facilitating guidance of the therapist. Our special populations are at home with the nonverbal communication inherent in motor activities. Movement is used to sustain and increase the attention obtained from the activities used in Stage I. Movement allows emotional expression when the movement is self-directed and accepted. Movement promotes body scheme because through movement, one becomes more aware of body parts and where they are in space; therefore, more aware of the physical self. Shifting, stretching, and rotating increases muscle tone so that we can behave more energetically. Good movement always stimulates better posture and balance, which in turn augments our sense of security and orientation in space. In this sense, movement becomes organizing.

This latter effect can be tested and observed immediately and continuously. Are group members able to follow how we are providing instructions? Do they need special help to get started, simpler instructions, or assistance in changing positions? Moving slowly, with verbal, visual, or physical cues, can all members perform simultaneously at least a few times within a given period? The therapist offers hands-on guidance as needed. As she does this, her action may be compared with verbal interaction that is provided by a therapist for clarification, understanding, and support. Group activity is promoted by good therapeutic touch (Ross, 1987, pg. 65).

Movement develops cohesiveness, that special feeling of sharing and belonging, that augments a sense of physical security. When everyone is doing the same thing together at the same time (eg,. holding on to one large object, watching someone demonstrating in the center, and imitating the perform-ance,) these actions can generate a special feeling of cohesiveness. This feeling of cohesiveness can be reinforced by holding hands or holding each other's elbows. It is promoted further by each member reaching forward with his special object, extending it into the center making physical contact with all the other similar objects. Clapping frequently for each other and offering praise also promotes connectedness.

Movement can address the needs of our populations to be either calmed or alerted. Usually, it is a mixture of both that is required, so it is of great importance for the therapist to respond using judgment and creativity. I respond to the dominant need that is apparent in the presenting group. When agitation, restlessness, and confusion prevail, I provide slow and more calming kind of movement (see Appendix) and distribute moderately heavy objects to be used by members. Novelty is introduced. My interactions will vary from benign ignoring to degrees of distancing. When sluggishness, isolation, some anxiety, indifference, or bewilderment prevails, then more alerting movements may be in order. For this kind of group, two or more objects may be passed around at separate times to be used in movement. I vary the objects so they are a mixture of light and heavy items to alert and calm. Little demand and fewer novel movements will be required of these members. My interactions with each individual will be brief and frequent.

It is important for the therapist to start where the patient is and not try to move too far from that status within any given session. For example, the therapist should not try to make a depressed group feel happy, but relief and support should be provided. The therapist considers overall physical condi-tion, specific disabling conditions, emotional needs, and cognitive function when selecting movement activities. More specifically:

1) *A way to encourage a positive response is to provide an object to each member for use during movement.* The object in the hand receives more attention than the way the hand is being used. The task becomes more automatic and irresistible. It is inner-directed and goal-directed, which can help one feel more in control. This works well with the most limited and physically involved group populations. The response appears organized and united as the therapist moves from one position to another, waiting, encouraging, and helping participants to perform. Each item is used differently as each presents different possibilities for use in a functional manner. Thus, movement can prepare or practice

functional patterns. This is elaborated on elsewhere as well as incorporated in some of the descriptions of the use of specific objects. New movements are born with different ways to use the body each time the item is brought to group and as members are watched for their own ingenious way to respond to the item. Bilateral use of the object is always encouraged, and using items is a good way to impose this natural way to use both sides of the body to work together.

Consider using objects, but changing the body position from sitting to a chair to sitting on the floor, a bench or standing. Stand on a block, inside a hoop, or sit on some type of vestibular board and new adaptations of the body are required with the use of any item. Suggestions are listed below:

- Batons
- Ribbons or streamers attached or tied to rods
- Chiffon scarves (Ross, 1987, p.87)
- Tiny bears or other tiny objects, ie, flower pots
- Tiny bears balanced on an inverted, small, plastic medicine cup
- Plates, ie, colorful, plastic, or microwave plates from frozen dinners, preferably not paper because it is too light
- Hand weights such as barbells or regular gym weights, 1/2 to 3 pounds (Ross, 1987, p.93)
- Nerf balls about 5 to 6 inches in diameter
- Plastic hollow rods, ie, containers for golf clubs
- Baskets, mixed sizes, but must have handles
- Flowers, paper or real
- Paper for wadding, then to be used in movement
- Chairs (Ross, 1987, p.89)
- Three-legged stools
- Leis or any long string of beads not easily broken
- Hoops (Ross, 1987, p.91)
- Rubber bands
- Soft bells (to ring or keep from ringing)
- Plastic soda bottle (2 liter) one third filled with sand, also may be used as bowling pins
- Balloons
- Rope about 3 feet long in length
- Bean bags, 2 to 3 ounces, about 3 x 3 inches
- Fli-Back, 10' plywood paddle with 1 1/4' diameter rubber ball (S & S Arts and Crafts)
- Musical instruments of any kind, ie, all marimbas, triangles, etc.
- Slinkies
- Fans, made or bought of paper and light wood
- Cones, two to each participant
- Stuffed dolls with moveable limbs

- Pantyhose or theraband about the same length

    The list is not inclusive. Some items become favorites and are used more often. When it is desirable for the group to hold onto one large object to encourage unity and focus, the following have been used:

- Rope; one 6 to 10 foot rope can be laid on the floor as a circle for establishing boundaries, for jumping into, walking on top of, having an inside circle of members facing an outside circle of members for working together, or just to have members hold onto in movement.

- Pantyhose circle; two pairs of pantyhose are tied to two more pairs until a large circle is formed. The knots are good handles to hold and sway. Put it around the backs of participants, leaving hands resting on it or free to exercise. Find ways to move feet using this stretchy material. This has been used with geriatric populations and physical disabilities. I have found it useful with young, highly distractible people. With the latter, as the tied hose encircles the back, they can turn around and lean into it without the tied hose circle falling away.

- Stretchy cloth; Handles sewn on the cloth are useful in helping members who may have a weak hand grasp or an inattentive member to hold on. While sitting on chairs arranged in a circle, start slowly with just waving the cloth, then raise cloth up higher and lower cloth down, then high enough to see all the others under the cloth, then place in back of the head. Repeat procedure. As cloth is held at knee height, kick feet high from under the cloth. Bounce a soft weight, (Ross, 1987, p.94).

Groups are planned more quickly when the equipment needed is at hand and easily chosen. Two recordings that offer versatility in rhythms have been used with all items. These are "Playtime Parachute Fun" and, especially, "Finger Play" (Kimbo); with only the instrumental side used. Contemporary music with a strong beat is also excellent.

Some initial suggestions for using the above items will be described, but this is not to be used as a limiting device for the reader. The principles involved are to introduce the object by starting with a simple way to hold it and then to move very slowly with object holding it in the prescribed way. Each movement is broken down to one step at a time so that an easy success is achieved. Waiting, without urging, to see that everyone is together is necessary. Principles are more important than methods because with use, both therapists and group members will discover more ways to use items than can be listed.

Consider, for example, how a plate may be used with music. It can be introduced and balanced on the palm of one hand, raised, lowered, brought to one shoulder and then to the other shoulder. It can be transferred to the other hand to imitate the same movements. The plate can be put around the back at waist level, transferred to the other hand, and brought around to the front at waist level, at knee level, or at neck level. Held with both hands, without moving feet, one can reach forward toward center, rotate to one side or the other. To isolate shoulder movement, which can be a difficult concept for some members, abduct arm horizontally and, with the plate on the palm of the hand, make a large circle in the air. Participants can balance the plate on their raised knee, or try balancing it on a bent elbow. Holding the plate as a waiter might, move into any position, such as stepping to the side or forward. Use it to catch a wad of paper another may throw. Members will contribute more ideas.

Consider how baskets may inspire novel ways to range the body. They should have handles and differ in sizes so that they can fit inside each other. Plunked down in the center of the group, people can choose the size they want. Group members can swing them on either side, twirl them, put them down and pick them up, hold with both hands and sway, hold them with only two fingers or one, with the wrist, with the elbow, and sometimes around the ear. Wear a basket as a hat. Walk into the center, meet someone, and exchange baskets. Rub for texture using the hands and arms. Ask who has the largest one, which requires everyone to look around. Allow the group to stack them, creating their own order and correcting their own mistakes.

Consider the possibilities that Nerf balls offer. These may be squeezed with palms opposing or with fingers digging in. They can be placed for squeezing under armpits, under thighs, between knees, and under chins. They can be pushed into and resisted by different parts of the body, rolled up and down the legs as both legs are placed together. Use one or all of the balls to toss to each other, or to play catch by oneself. Use balls as something for the hands to hold as participants move across midline, in diagonal patterns, or to reach and bend.

Consider how the Fli Ball, a small rubber ball attached with an elastic string to a wooden paddle, can reinforce meaningful function in a group. It is generations old, yet it remains contemporary. It can encourage bilateral coordination, midline crossing, motor planning, spatial relations, body scheme, and auditory and visual processing. If used as intended, it requires a great deal of skill in eye-hand coordination, and some may be able to do it. This is hard to expect. Using the principles mentioned earlier, have participants hold the paddle in front of them. The dangling ball dances to music and, as the group does this together, it looks like dancing puppets. Raised or lowered slowly, it becomes a challenge not to get one rubber string caught with others, which can bring laughter and more self awareness. From Barbara Panzer, OTR/L, comes the suggestion that the rubber string be placed around the neck of the participant. Then holding the rubber about 6 inches from the ball with the left hand, use the paddle with the right hand to rhythmically hit the ball to music. This can be tried by changing sides so that the left hand paddles the ball. Bounce the ball behind someone, or, if the group is ambulatory, walk in a small circle bouncing ball. Have the group turn the paddle with one hand to wrap the rubber around the paddle and then unwrap it. There is a good amount of weight shifting and total body movement in the accomplishment of these steps. Special populations find it fun once they are guided into successful results with it and other movements evolve.

The placing of objects in the hands of participants in the movement stage has demonstrated the following. Stroke patients in groups can perform more bilateral movements with items in their hands, despite flaccidity in one hand, as holding the item chiefly requires shoulder movement. Placing objects in the hands of persons with Alzheimer's disease promotes their greater participation. The population considered retarded make it an opportunity to catch up on new experiences and grow innovative.

2) *Breathing activities for relaxation and oxygenation.*
   a. Hold up the index finger and feel your breath as you blow on it.
   b. Use a pinwheel regularly.
   c. Hold a feather and blow on it.
   d. Blow a ping pong ball onto a piece of a cardboard that has been cut to resemble a doughnut. Make the inner empty space very large to accommodate the ball. Or blow the ball across the table to another group member.
   e. Place a puddle of tempera paint on paper. Blow through a straw and spread the paint in different directions.
   f. Use party blowers, whistles, or plastic kazoos to hum a tune. Kazoos can be sterilized for reuse.
   g. Blow soap bubble solutions, bought or made, with pipes or special rings. Try to hold, count, or catch bubbles.
   h. Group members often lack sufficient strength to blow up a balloon. Consider asking them to do this periodically if they are unable to succeed at this session. Just keeping the balloon bouncing from the right to left hand for the duration of a piece of music can be a triumph.
   i. Instruction and exploration of breathing techniques for relaxation can be offered. Take a deep breath, hold it, and slowly exhale with the mouth open. Make kissing or other noises with the mouth. Ask participants to place palms together, take a deep breath, push palm against palm, and exhale slowly. Techniques for using imagery to reduce tension can be found to work well in a group (Siegal, 1987). A modified technique of the Quieting Reflex, developed by a Hartford psychiatrist Charles Stroebel, is as follows: breathe out, shaping mouth like "O'; breathe in, smile inwardly; think, "alert mind, calm body'; exhale, let jaw, tongue, shoulders go loose, allow feeling of warmth and looseness to flood through the body as tension flows out through toes. Do this several times with group members so that they may take this exercise with them to practice as often as possible during the day to relieve tension.

3) *Primary and brief motor activities*
   a. Group particiants often are in crouched, flexed, or hunched positions. Starting where the group is, ask members to cross their arms and hug themselves (help them if necessary), then to touch the air on either side by extending their arms and return to a hugging position. This permits their safe return to the initial position, but some change has been felt and movement for more body extension becomes possible.
   b. Provide each participant with a bracelet. Each bracelet should be different (eg, hard, wide, narrow, stiff, or limp) and be constructed of wood, plastic, metal, or other material. The therapist approaches each group member with a dowel similar to the one used in ring toss. The therapist changes the position of the dowel from high to low, left to right, and near to far, or on top of a group member's head. Emphasis is placed how well the participant locates and reaches placement. Group members are invited to take the place of the therapist.
   c. Participants are provided with a paper cup to place on the floor at their feet. Participants circle the cup with each foot separately and slowly with at least toes touching the floor. Push cup forward, bring it back. Push the cup to the side and return it. Shifting in the chair becomes necessary and automatic to maintain balance. At the end, the cup can be squashed with feet. Some require several cups because they enjoy the last step so much.
   d. Parachute play with king sized sheets or regular parachutes are enjoyed by chairbound and other nonambulatory participants (Kimbo catalogue).
   e. Group participants have displayed with smiles and laughter their enjoyment of vestibular stimulation or movement of the head in space. That which can be provided in a linear plane is more acceptable to the majority of participants, and is recommended in the literature. Rocking, swaying, or swinging provide this stimulation within a group format. For example, sitting in a swing and aiming a bean bag at a target is fun to watch and do. Choose a large enough target so that mastery by the majority of members is assured by the third attempt. Slow vestibular stimulation tends to relax and calm; fast, prolonged vestibular stimulation is not recommended as it can cause dizziness or breathlessness. Especially when providing vestibular stimulation, the therapist proceeds with caution and very careful modifications may be introduced quickly. Activities that provide acceleration and deceleration in movements of the head in space, such as the scooter board, have been offered to the neurologically involved, psychiatric adult as well as to the adults with mental

retardation. Propelling themselves or being pulled by another was seen as very enjoyable activities in a small group. A 60 inch x 30 inch vestibular board can be used for slow rocking in supine or other positions. Doing individual activities such as these require a demonstration period where group members watch and select what they wish to experience. Small groups can use the equipment under staff's careful supervision. Such stimulation has not been provided by this therapist on a continuous and regular basis but as a part of a sequence of activities offered to the group. Whenever equipment was available and offered to group participants, it was received with much enjoyment and a session where goals were achieved always ensued.

4) *Moderately advanced activities*

   a. Plan movement so that participants can feel how the body responds. Provide names for the muscles in action. Do this by proceeding in a developmental manner, first turning the neck from one side to the other side showing group members how to do this with hands placed around the neck feeling the musculature that is moving. Avoid circular rotation around the neck. Put hands on the stomach and back to feel flexion and extension. Put a hand on the shoulder while raising and lowering arm. Place one hand on the scapula as it is protracted and retracted on that side. Do the same with all joints of the arm and legs. Experience and experiment with all the different ways the joints can move. The fine joints of fingers and hands can be explored by spreading fingers and pushing and pulling each finger.

   b. Distribute large sheets of newspaper. With one hand starting at one corner, ask participants to crumble the sheet into a wad. Repeat with the other hand. Squeeze wad together with both hands and use as a toss game.

   c. Raising the hands high, tear a newspaper into strips. Group members can be instructed that for easy tearing, the paper should be torn from top to bottom. Useful craft projects start with these strips.

   d. Pick up marbles with the toes, or crumple a paper towel placed on the floor, also with the toes. Direct group participants in the activity of tracing the pattern of their own or partner's feet on a large sheet of paper. Label foot drawings with correct names and hang them on the wall. Who has the widest foot, longest foot, or shortest toes?

   e. With one body part, ask each participant to touch as many other body parts as possible. For example, use the right elbow to touch both hips, knees, the left wrist, right ankle, right ear, etc. Try the same with the smallest finger, the nose, and the big toe.

   f. Ball activity can engender leadership skills. The selected leader stands in the center of a circle and throws the ball to each member individually, who have to respond by throwing it back to the leader.

This is sometimes very hard to understand for some group members, who may want to throw it randomly, as well as for the member who acts as leader. When each member has been so contacted, a new leader comes into the center and rolls the ball to each member. The ball can be handed, dribbled, bounced once or twice, or kicked gently. A song can be sung with this. The therapist may have to have assistance so that members can be helped sufficiently to achieve success.

g. Using a rope in movement was suggested in the beginning of this chapter. Additional activities for its use are as follows: Place a 10 foot rope on the floor so participants can walk on top of the rope with eyes open or closed, jump zigzag from side to side, or walk on one side of the rope and back the other side (forward or backward). Designs can be made on the floor with rope by wiggling one end. The rope can be tied between two chairs as participants step over it with great care for safety. When tied higher up on the chairs, it can signify a volleyball net.

h. Mat work is recommended, especially if it can be made into a cooperative endeavor rather than each member doing his own thing. A game of passing an object with hands or feet, and having it timed, provides rolling, reaching, raising, and maneuvering in space so as not to bump others. Experimenting, one at a time, the many different ways one can get across a long mat always brings out unexpected creativity as does "follow the leader" across the mat. These are in addition to the first activity suggested in this chapter, where sitting on the floor with an object to use in movement will alter the way the body has to respond in using the object in that kind of sitting position.

i. A circular formation fosters support and cohesiveness among members of the group. Participants can give support to each other by holding hands and, therefore, be better able to stand on one foot, hop, jump, and perform other actions such as circling right and left, walking to the center and out to the edge, etc. Any type of folk dancing that may be achieved is very good in promoting the goals of alerting and calming. Once the feeling of cohesiveness appears to prevail, line formation, such as that required in a Virginia Reel, can be attempted (Kimbo, KIM 0860 "Dances for Little People"). This is easier to accomplish than square dancing.

j. See how many universal gestures you can express with your hands. Examples might be "no," "come on," "goodbye," "go away," "quiet," "money," "rock-a-bye baby," "praying," and "peace." Participants will suggest more than the therapist can imagine. Discuss how each individual has used his hands during his life. Demonstrate in pantomime.

k. Postures can be assumed by the participants that represent a prayerful posture, a gesture that expresses anger or happiness, etc. The posture of joy is extension, abduction, and external rotation of limbs such as in the Degas painting, "The Ballet Dancer." Postures and movements that improve oxygenation affect the mood so that one may feel happier just by changing a bodily position. (Ross, 1987).

l. A freeze game is suggested that initiates good movement, auditory reception, ability to follow directions, and stay on task. Have group members practice saying the word "freeze" in unison. Then, a simple action pattern such as hand clapping, knee slapping, or marching in place is introduced and practiced until most can do this, to some degree, together. When the therapist says "freeze," group members stop the action. This should be practiced several times. To raise the level of this activity, a few ambulatory members can go to the center of the circle and perform walking, twisting, or other axial movements while others continue with the original hand clapping. At the signal, both groups attempt to stop moving and hold the position. It may be necessary to cue and individually help group members. Music can be played and group members are instructed to freeze when they no longer hear the music. Much praise is offered for success.

m. Balance beams can be purchased or constructed with blocks of wood placed on the floor, a 6 foot strip of heavy cardboard or a long piece of carpeting for group members to walk on top of. Difficulties that need to be addressed with therapeutic knowledge and assistance will be observed. Walking can be varied by walking backward, sideways, fast, slow, and balancing on one foot. Arm movements, such as swinging, shaking, clapping, reaching, punching, or waving, can also be added.

Your Own Suggestions Below:

CHAPTER 3

Stage III
Visual Motor
Perceptual Activities

In this stage, tasks are offered that require less physical and more thoughtful action. Such tasks can be identifying, and interpreting sensory data in a more precise manner than was required during the previous stage. Selected activities should elicit productive, meaningful, or corrective responses. This stage is used to tone down the physical exertion and excitement created in Stage II, as tasks require more reflective thought and planned motor response.

Perception, as used in this manual, is the awareness and interpretation of the physical world as we relate to it. It is influenced by the feedback messages of movement and stimuli received from all sensory systems. Memory processes and emotional associations also are evoked. "Perception is viewed as the personal, subjective, and sometimes puzzling process by which a person actively searches and judges the external environment" (Abreu, 1981 as cited in Abreu, and Toglia, 1987). "The process of perception includes sensory detection, sensory analysis, hypothesis formation, and a decision response" (Klatzy, 1980 as cited by Abreu, and Toglia, 1987). Perception works with cognition, as perception is considered the ability to process and interpret information. Cognition involves this and contributes even more processes to a successful response to sensory information. (Abreu and Toglia, 1987).

The thrust of the Five-Stages is that as the participant feels safe, secure, accepted, successful in his actions, and experiences more energy, he wants to, and is able to, perform better. He can perform tasks that if presented earlier, either would not have held his interest or would have required too much energy to accomplish. Fundamental conditions must be in place, more so for special populations than others, for adaptive, appropriate actions to take place.

It is very important to present tasks in this stage that can be achieved successfully by the majority of participants within two to four attempts. This helps the therapist know that the task was appropriately selected because it resulted in a learning experience. Chapter 9 ("Conducting a Group") discusses the need for the therapist to think about presenting a task in a progressively graded manner, upwards or downwards, so that the presentation is correlated with the functional level of the group members. Although this is important in all the stages, it is imperative in Stage III as group cohesiveness is building and is tenuous. Group members show satisfaction with success as they usually say, "I can't do that," then try and find they succeed. They often display verbal and motor responses that are not forthcoming in routine caregiving as a result of their good feeling.

Chapter 7 ("Relevance of Theoretical Treatment Approaches") discusses the necessity to call upon all relevant references as a base for knowledge in selecting, creating, and presenting activities for groups. Perceptual tasks used in the treatment of learning disabilities, traumatic brain injuries, and other central nervous system injuries or diseases are appropriate.

The new activity introduced in this stage sustains or regains the awareness, alertness, and attentiveness of group members in a natural way just as with any shift in action. Group cohesiveness grows with watching, learning, and performing to the extent that a therapist is realistic about the capabilities of group participants to grow in awareness. This means that the therapist becomes very sensitive to very subtle but meaningful behavioral changes observed while working with members of special populations. Some of the changes seen in participants include their ability to begin making eye contact, a willingness to be guided by touch, ability to pass an item with one or no cue, to sit erect without losing earlier positioning, and to make more than one attempt at an activity. This stage requires some risk taking, judgment, and decision making, followed by physical action and a visible, successful, and enjoyable outcome. Any combination or variety of choices from this category is satisfactory; however, it must be balanced against the movement chosen. If the latter has been strenuous, choose the less physically active perceptual activity. Suggested activities are described as follows:

1) Games using items to throw with accuracy can be constructed or purchased. The target may be a large or small container or a spot marked on the ground or perpendicular to participants. Objects to throw may be wadded paper, different kinds and sizes of balls, bean

bags, safe darts, rolled socks, scarves, a soft toy, a prickly item such as an acorn, and so on. Adapt the game "Twister" by tossing a bean bag on the color indicated by the spinner.

2) Races that can be competitive between two or more groups can be traditional or original considering material at hand. Using different colored plastic cones or different textured cones, a variety of games can be created. Teams can be lined up and asked to go one at a time. Each participant is given a cone. The participant is required to match his cone with the appropriate cone placed 6 feet away. Start this game by asking participants to practice piling all cones on top of one cone placed 6 feet away in front of each team. Players learn about speed, distance, directionality, coordinating movement, and moving and competitive activity. This game is successful with the developmentally disabled population.

3) Group members can shine a flashlight around the room using the beam to locate objects, make designs, and land on a part of someone's anatomy.

4) Use any game that will encourage pointing: "I see something in this room that goes up and down," (window shade); "that goes on and off"; "that cannot be moved"; "that goes all around"; "that makes a consistent sound"; "that is transparent"; and so on.

5) Using skills of matching, directionality, eye-hand coordination:
   a. Draw a human figure on a large poster board. Superimpose a duplicate figure cut up into parts. Group should learn to name body parts, side, and plane (Appendix).
   b. Placement of blocks or shapes can be worked on top of a design of blocks or shapes. The design can be placed on a tray held in the therapist's hands, laid on a table, or put on the floor (Appendix).
   c. Use 3- to 5-foot puzzles, and construct them on the table or floor (Appendix).
   d. Use peg boards with graded cards outlining a design to be copied (Appendix).
   e. Passing items left and right around a group circle can be incorporated with other goals. Articles may be selected for their touch/tactile input, proprioceptive input, ability to evoke reminiscences, and to promote social contact.

6) Using skills of form constancy:
   a. Use tongue depressor shapes (Appendix). Construct shapes using different color construction paper so that shapes or colors may be matched. Participants take one or two shapes and the therapist holds up a shape. Group members holding that shape raise their hand, do some action, or go into the center of the circle and wave the shape. Disregarding shape, the therapist can choose to call

colors and the same responses can be given. Group members can take the place of the therapist by calling out a shape or color. When performed with music at an even pace, it may seem like a preplanned dance.

b. Play the game: "I am thinking of something in this room that is..." round, square, etc, and substitute color, size, etc.

7) Estimate distance and weights:

a. Estimate the number of steps the therapist or a group member needs to take to a predetermined place or between two objects. Make up other problems to solve. Measure arm length or leg circumference of a volunteer group member.

b. Measure items close and distant to group members to gauge whether perspective is understood. First use larger measurements such as the height of a door, the circumference of a table, the surface area of a picture or wall hanging, and then add the concepts of near and far. Then follow with small items such as pencils, books, etc.

c. Weigh different items on a scale. "Does this look heavier than that?" Any scale, even a food scale, will do.

8) Figure Ground Activities:

a. Distinguish one scent from another. With geriatric groups, choose only one or two scents to pass around and have some dialogue about it. Pass around perfume, mustard, vanilla, vinegar, or other strong scents for guessing and comparing. Scents in a liquid preparation are easier to distinguish than dried versions of the same scent. Some strong-smelling candles have delightful shapes and colors to touch and see, thus stimulating many senses at once. Participants who are regressed may be able only to identify a scent as something they like or do not like. A pungent smell, such as an onion or garlic, or a cotton ball soaked in almond or lemon flavoring may be used to collect and alert the group in this stage. The therapist may ask, "Did you like that scent? How is it used? When did you use it?" If the participant is given an almond cookie or lemonade immediately following, perhaps some association can be made and the flavoring can be distinguished. Scents are important as they can be immediately alerting, irritating, or relaxing. This feeling can be put to work to produce action in another activity, whether it be a follow-up activity or going on to another stage in group procedure.

b. When one can obtain packets of powdered lemon, powdered milk, and sugar, samples of all three can be placed on individual napkins in the same sequence, with participants guessing by taste which item is on the right, in the middle, and on the left.

c. Group members can identify sounds on tapes or records loaned from public libraries. There is a variety of industrial, animal, transportation, environmental, and atmospheric sounds, but there are also opportunities to distinguish the horn from other traffic noises or one instrument from a host of others. Use the sounds as background for a game that can be played by passing a bean bag around from member to member until the record stops. The person holding the bean bag may be considered as "out" of the game. Play until all members are out.

d. Pictures may be hung around the room and group members asked to search for the largest one, the one with a cat in it, or similar themes. Place the pictures high, low ,and in novel places. Pictures should be large, colorful, and easily identifiable.

e. Any figure ground test may be put on poster board and used as a group activity. This is greatly enjoyed by all populations. All table top paper and pencil exercises can be enlarged to poster board size and, therefore, be better able to be seen by the whole group.

f. Puzzles are elaborated on in Chapter 8.

g. Activities and games that involve following a pattern, finishing lines, and finding the sequence are recommended. These activities can also be put on blackboard or poster board.

h. See Pictorial Review of a Five-Stage Group, Stage III.

i. Cut out a board of any shape about the size of the usual cutting board. I have one representing, in outline, a short boot. Hammer nails in it randomly. Group participants are given either colored rubber bands or colored loopers and requested to hook one end around a nail and stretch it as far as possible in a straight line to hook around another nail. Eventually it becomes an abstract design with colored lines. This task can be made more difficult as participants are asked to take squares and triangles and move more into each other's spaces, creating an even nicer abstract. People can help each other. This activity has been used with very low functioning populations. It can sometimes be appropriate to discuss abstract design as compared with realistic pictures. Examples of different art work can be introduced and this may flow naturally into Stage IV.

j. Make your own dominoes on cards measuring 5 x 8 inches. Use them on the floor or a large table. Draw a line down the center of the cards, allowing for two spaces for two different symbols or a blank space. Draw domino symbols using dots numbering from one to six, or use flowers to match or any other item of which a sufficient number of copies may be obtained. Play by the egular rules for matching, but allow each group member only one card.

Trying to match one card makes it easier to understand what is expected. The therapist may have to practice this many times with the group before it can be accomplished in an orderly way. A version of "Concentration" may also be played with these cards.

9) Touch discrimination and tactile stimulation activities

   a. Test temperature discrimination with hot and cold vials on upper and lower parts of the body. Hot and cold packs may be passed around along with other items chosen for contrast and comparison.

   b. Lightly touch the shoulder, arm, knee, or back of participants who have their eyes closed. Can they tell if and where they are touched?

   c. Explore items of various textures by passing around little boards with sample textures glued on. When each board has a match, a game of matching with eyes closed or open can be conducted. Place many items in a container or bag in which participants go "fishing" for a requested hard, soft, smooth, rough, sharp, heavy, or light object. If items are all able to be manipulated and make a sound, a change in shape, or an air puff, request that members figure out how this happens by manipulating the item. Fill container with sand, beans, oats, or rice and ask participants to locate and identify familiar objects that are hidden. This is best done with a small group so behaviors can be monitored. Well-wrapped treats can be hidden and then kept by the participants. This may be introduced to the group as exercise for the small joints. Under the rubric of exercise for the small joints, participants can be given plastic pieces to join together in designs, remove twist ties on baggies holding a treat, open jars to remove an item and then replace the cap, slice fruit, or open a zippered container such as a small pea pod pillow, and remove the contents and then replace it. The latter activities can all be tried using just one hand as well.

10) Bilaterality and body scheme reinforcement:

   a. Rhythmic training can begin by using one hand or body part on one side of the body and progress to two hands and alternating body sides. Tap the chair tray with one hand, clap, stamp feet, beat sticks to music in different rhythms. Tap out the rhythm of one's first and last name. Use rhythmic combinations in sequence, such as four claps, four stamps, four hand shakes, or four knee slaps. Music may be added.

   b. The player tries to catch rings thrown to him on two pieces of doweling, one held in each hand. Rings are thrown so the player must move forward, left, right, high, or low. For those players unable to use doweling, a hoop may be held in the air and they may toss a bean bag through the hoop. Choices can be offered to participants.

c. The following activity is offered in a graded sequence:
   1. Identification of body parts:
      a) The therapist touches different body parts and says, "This is my head: touch your head." Continue, using mouth ears, chin, neck, shoulders, arms, elbows, wrists, hands, fingers, chest, stomach, hips, legs, knees, ankles, feet, and toes. Use more sophisticated language such as thigh, calf, or even name muscles with more advanced groups.
      b) Ask the group to touch body parts on command, ie, "Place both hands on your head."
      c) Repeat b, with the eyes closed.
      d) Have the group touch body parts with other body parts such as: nose to knee, ear to shoulder, fingers to shoulder, toes to heel, and elbow to stomach.
   2. Focus on body parts:
      a) Ask the group members to imitate movements of the therapist such as "Nod your head, close your eyes, twist your neck, bend your elbows, clap your hands, wiggle your toes, open your mouth, shrug your shoulders, snap your fingers, bend your knees, and stamp your feet."
      b) Repeat (a) but do not demonstrate.
      c) The therapist states the usage of a body part and group members supply the name: "I see with my ____, I talk with my ____, I walk with my ____, I think with my ____."
   3. Body image exercises:
      a) Draw a person, draw oneself, or draw one's feet in outline standing on a sheet of clean newsprint.
      b) Draw an incomplete person on the blackboard and have members supply the missing parts.
   4. Use games to reinforce body parts such as Simon Says, Looby Loo, Hokey Pokey, Red Light, and Pin the Nose on the Pumpkin or Bow on the Dressed-Up Lady or Man cutout.
   5. Pass around a mirror and ask participants to state which feature they liked best on themselves. Create a discussion as members are asked to remember what others in the group have said, are asked for suggestions, agreement, or what others in the past may have said. Have the mirror go around again for another good look.
   6. Use action poems to encourage movement response. The words can be chanted along with the movement. The following are suggestions:

I

Hands on your hips, hands on your knees, put them behind you if you please; Touch your shoulders, touch your nose, touch your knees, touch your toes. Now you raise them way up high, let your fingers swiftly fly; Put them out in front of you, clap one two, one two.

Hands upon your head now place, touch your shoulders, wash your face; Raise them up high like before, Now we clap one, two, three, four.

II

Let's all stand straight and tall, raise hands high, let them fall. Touch your ears, touch your nose, touch your hair, touch your toes. Touch your shoulders, touch your hips, touch your knees, touch your lips. Stretch your arms out far and wide, now let fall gently to your side.

III

Touch your nose, touch your chin, that's the way we will begin; Touch your eyes, touch your knees, now pretend you're going to sneeze; Touch your hair, touch your ear, touch your two red lips right here; Touch your elbows where they bend, that's the way this touch game ends.

IV

Roll, roll, roll your hands as slowly as can be; Roll, roll, roll your hands, do it now with me. Repeat. Add other actions such as: Clap, clap, clap your hands. Shake, shake, shake your hands. Stamp, stamp, stamp your feet. Nod, nod, nod your head.

7. Pantomime drama uses motor planning and imagination. Select a theme, such as making a garden. Group members describe sequentially what must be done to make a garden. Act out in exercise manner such related gardening actions as: spade the ground, make a furrow for seeds, drop in seeds, rake, hoe, pick up stones and throw in a pile, pull up weeds and throw in a pile, pick vegetables, flowers, etc.

   "Chores of winter" or "Winter in the old days": view falling snow, walk in heavy snow, shovel snow, ice skate, make a snowman, throw snowballs, rub cold body parts to get warm.

   Encourage group members to remember themes from past experiences and use this for group discussion. Make up other themes appropriate to holidays, morning chores, etc. This can be combined with Stage IV in reflecting on feelings and sharing with others.

11) A novel way of tapping imaginations or introducing reality is to show a creatively designed item (eg, a pencil that sharpens itself, a carrying bag that turns into a footstool or bring in a bag of groceries) or find an article (eg, on quilting) with a sample piece for group members to handle. Price, creative uses, and material can be explored in many ways.

12) Place a basin of water on an area covered by newspapers. Group members can throw plastic objects into the basin with sufficient force to splash out the water. Place a hoop in the water and throw items to land within the hoop.

13) Putting (as in golf) using an electric receptacle (on the market) that returns the ball can be a successful activity with the most regressed population. Use a strip of carpeting, about 8 feet long, place the electric putter at one end of the carpet, and give a putting iron and three golf balls to a participant. Participants should watch each other take turns. This encourages focusing, motor planning, relating to space, scanning, and tracking. Gratification is immediate.

14) A wooden ladder can be placed on the floor in the center of the group circle. Bean bags, Nerf balls, erasers, and knotted socks can be passed around the circle as group members are encouraged to squeeze and feel these objects. Group interaction is facilitated by therapist modeling a smile, nod, touch, eye contact, hello, or a thank you. One at a time, objects can be thrown to land in between the rungs of a ladder.

15) The Forward Pass (DLM) (a football with two ropes passing through it) and used by two or four people is recommended. Both young and old will want to try it. The ropes can be shortened at the handle to accommodate the possibility of limited strength in upper extremity. It is used with coordinated bilateral shoulder abduction and adduction movements and requires that partners cooperate to continue. Participants learn from watching as they wait for their turn.

16) Two pictures of similar subject matter can be compared and discussed. Each group may manifest a special interest, such as always responding favorably to pictures of babies, animals, or nature. Three dimensional pictures that when turned slightly appear as if they are moving may spark a response. Musical cards and books are available with interesting three dimensional scenes. Passing and handling these items are essential; when it is not possible to allow handling, these should not be shown.

17) Computers and robots have a multitude of uses for all populations. Robots come in a great variety. An excellent article (McLean, 1988) demonstrates the use of many kinds of robots in a group setting using the Five-Stages. Chapter 8 ("Conducting the Five-Stage Group")

refers to using a robot with low functioning, severely disabled students. Radio Shack is one source for obtaining robots and other suggestions are provided under Resources. Supplies for constructing switches for all uses may also be obtained from Radio Shack.

A group of young adults with moderate retardation were fascinated with a demonstration of how a battery-operated toy could be activated by a lever and a mercury switch. This group then handled a board with four cutout shapes consisting of a square, circle, triangle, and rectangle. The board had been wired so that it could be activated as a switch for the same battery-operated toy when the last shape was placed into its correct space. They were stimulated to ask more questions than usual as they experimented with exploring how each switch worked.

Computers also, can be used in a group format with these populations. A large amount of appropriate software (see Resources) is available for computers. Occupational therapists are writing introductory articles on computers and their uses in the *Occupational Therapy Journal, News, Forum*, and *Advance* (See Bibliography). Software that require choices to be made by hitting any key or other method that does not require knowing letters can be used with a group. All levels of appropriate software exist for groups. Problem solving and decision making skills are required in a fun atmosphere as members use a program to bake a cake on screen, score with successful answers, or create a design. Programs run the gamut of visual motor perceptual skills. Motor, perceptual, cognitive, and social objectives can be achieved when considering the use of computers, robots, and switches.

Your Own Suggestions Below:

CHAPTER *4*

Stage IV
Cognitive Stimulation and Functioning

In this stage, the therapist guides members to use the energy generated in the previous stages to focus on a cognitive task. This is the opportune time for group members to demonstrate their optimum level of thoughtful and creative self-expression as they are involved with themselves and each other while doing an activity. Stage IV can be the high point of cohesiveness and sharing, and it becomes the best time for encouraging relevant verbalization. This is the time when mastery in relating to others and to the environment is at its best as observed by self-imposed boundaries, posture, self-expression and focus on a common task. *This is the time to remember any issue that was postponed for discussion at the beginning of the group.* Emotions are less intense, more involvement of group membership is secured, and the resolution often happens by itself as the group member will suggest his own solution as if he had been working on it throughout the session. As a result, the therapist can often be less involved. With more reserve on her part, members sometimes choose to take more responsibility. The therapist may have to provide the direction by introducing the activity. Sometimes members provide clues as to what is needed, and then the activity is changed to suit the needs.

Cognition and communication can proceed from the perceptual task of the previous stage as there is no fine line of where one ends and the other begins. It can be a natural outflow to process in this stage what members were doing in the previous stage. The therapist can ask for a description of what was just done, how it felt to do it, what the participant learned about himself, what was the objective of the activity, or simply whether it should be done the same way again. Any or all of these aspects can encompass Stage IV. Some of the activities suggested below for this stage may be suitable for starting in Stage III. Then it may be appropriate to continue, to review the activity in Stage IV, and talk about the purpose of the activity. Additional activities to consider using in Stage IV are as follows:

1) Poetry can be used in diverse ways. Principles of poetry therapy can be incorporated here: the therapist can facilitate individual or group created poetry. Short verses of created poetry written in large letters can be distributed to group members to be read one line a piece, a whole stanza, or read together and then read again. Contrasting poems relating to feelings, past experiences, and beliefs are conducive to group discussion. Group members can choose roles to read out loud from poems that have dialogues within their verses.

2) Creative storytelling techniques, reminiscence, riddles, and jokes can be introduced. Whatever can be made as visual, tactile or concrete as possible will aid the associations needed to emerge for group members to participate to the fullest. For example, start a story with "The night was dark. The barn door creaked." Or, "Tell us about your favorite teacher." Looking around in a room, therapist can ask, "What goes all around and never moves? Up and down? (Window blind) Off and On? Has four legs but never walks? Carries sound but never talks?"

3) Use a tape recorder. Replay conversations, recitations, and encourage talking into the tape recorder when it is accepted by group members. The replay must be clear or it can cause frustration and scatter attention.

4) Exercise the mind with memory games.
   a. Review the sequence of activities done during the session. Cues can be used according to the needs of group members.
   b. Display two to three familiar items. Cover items with a cloth (See Chapter 11). Guess what they are. This can be upgraded in many ways: items may be increased; allow for a time lapse before guessing; or introduce one novel item that presents little association with the others can be introduced. Memory games should be played with sensitivity as they are not meant to hold up the mirror to losses but to be used as a means to prod and improve memory skills. Do not subject the group to what cannot be accomplished by most members. For example, with some groups, remembering

names without constant cueing can never be achieved and this must be accepted.

    c. Play a game of concentration on the floor or on a table. For example, use pictures of large single flowers from two of the same catalogues so that two matching cards may be made up. Make pairs of pictures of tools, cars, expressive babies, or jewelry.

    d. Use a container to hide an item so that weight and sound may be used to guess what is hidden. For example, there are paper mache egg-shaped containers of all sizes. Prepare two sets of four items such as, a small bell, 1 inch sponge cube, a rock, and a safety pin or paper clip. I model putting one item (from one set of four items hidden from the group) in the container and passing it around for all to handle. The duplicate set of the four items is laid out in a row for members to view. Group members handle the closed container and guess the item that is hidden. Then one member is given a set of four items and chooses which one of the items he will hide so that group members cannot see his choice. He is helped to do this if he cannot manage alone. Then the closed container is passed around from member to member to handle, shake, and guesses are made as to which of the four items displayed might have been hidden. To upgrade this activity, close the gap between weights by including a heavy rubber band that makes a small sound, include more choices, or do not display the duplicate set. Therapist should be aware of all the good movements required by this activity that challenge posture and balance with coordinated hand use, in addition to the visual and auditory discrimination, attentiveness, and cognition required. Especially in this kind of activity, which may be demanding of some group members, the therapist helps members to acquire tolerance for patient waiting. Also, any behavior can be processed with the group during or after the activity for validity or reinforcement.

5) An interesting picture can induce a mood and initiate reflection. For example, seasonal or unseasonal pictures of weather conditions, holidays, or pictures of children's faces are introduced. These pictures need to be uncluttered and can be expressive of a wide range of emotions from happiness to sadness, from impudence to innocence or from whatever else you choose that is appropriate and evocative. Either one picture is displayed for discussion or a series of pictures are shown for the purpose of guessing the season, holiday, or an emotion depending on the objective behind the activity.

6) Show and tell. Bring items from home such as a collection of photographs, souvenirs, hobby collections, or even food (eg, a pineapple). Items can be passed around to be handled and discussed.

Members can calculate the cost of a bag of groceries, sporting goods items, toys, or clothes the therapist has introduced. Encourage the group to bring pictures of family members, birthday cards, or personal possessions they might have.

7) Encourage the group to share with and care for each other. A dialogue between members is precious. This is how a group facilitates learning from each other's wisdom. Members need practice to respond to each other, and this may be assisted by exercises that begin: "Tell us about a favorite school teacher." (Talicor; see Resources) "Look at your neighbor and notice something"; "Say something nice about the person next to you"; "Say something nice about yourself." Start a topic with: "I appreciate", "I wish," or "What makes you happy... or what memory makes you happy?" Allow time for members to respond and even disagree with each other or offer another point of view. The therapist can go around the group and state the positive observations that may be made about each member on his participation in the session.

8) Show a 10-minute slide presentation on any subject of general interest to the group. Popcorn may accompany this.

9) Blackboard activities can be done on the lap or an upright board.

   a. "I wish" statement can be written on the board and the list can be read in entirety at the end.

   b. Each member can write his name where he wishes on the board. The therapist may summarize this activity by remarking, "There is room and a place for everyone and each can choose where it will be."

   c. Fill a lap blackboard with at least five rows of single-digit numbers Each group member can be given a different task. One can put a circle around all 3's, another underscores all 1's and another can put brackets when he finds two numbers, in any direction, that add up to 5, and so on. A member can be asked to cross out any number that begins with a vowel when it is spelled. All numbers remaining untouched can be checked off by members, one at a time, as the board goes around again.

   d. Put sequential numbers or letters on various parts of the board. Members must draw the connecting line that shows the sequence. Colored chalk may be used.

   e. Simple objects may be drawn leaving a part removed for group members to draw in or correct. Distort a picture, such as draw a fish extending out of a fish bowl. Design a tree with leaves or a bush with flowers for group members to choose a leaf or flower on which to write their name.

   f. Each member may draw an item and a story may be concocted with

Figure 4-1. There's a lot of action in the sea. The octopus is swimming with the fish. The little fish is in the fish's tummy. The big fish ate the little fish. The sun came out and we got a nice day on the sea. The bird is flying through the cloud. There is an octopus, serpent on the boat. I like the picture; everybody made the picture. Everything is down at the seashore; I wouldn't mind being there. By Tues. a.m. group.

        cueing by therapist, or each member can use colored chalk to create a design that can flow together with the others. The colored chalk differentiates each individual's contribution to the total design.

    g.   Any appropriate paper and pencil game, eg, hangman or supplying the missing word to proverbs, can be presented.

10) The use of music is very appropriate. The re-introduction of a music box or choosing to distribute tambourines to keep the beat while listening to music depends on what is needed by the group. Presenting live music, music to be appreciated, music with a theme for a holiday, or music for relaxing are just a few ways to use this special modality. Somehow the group members have to be brought into this activity with music as an integral part of the presentation if only they strum once, hum once, or assume a position or action sometime during the few minutes of this part of the group session. The group members are participants in the session. Presentation is not used here to present an entertainment program but to invite participation and involvement from each group member.

12) Construct a felt board out of a large flattened cardboard box and cover

it with felt. As illustrated in the Figure above, felt objects can dramatize an impromptu story, reconstruct the items and parts of a room, (eg, bedroom or kitchen), or serve as a visual aid for group discussions. They may be used to review shapes, colors, sizes, and categories, (eg, fruits and vegetables, the four seasons, or the four food groups). Glue any paper picture to a piece of felt, which then can be attached to the felt board as if it were a felt piece.

Your Own Suggestions Below:

CHAPTER *5*

Stage V
Closing the Session

In this stage, brief activities are appropriate so that the benefits of accomplishment and equilibrium may be experienced by group members. In terms of group dynamics, the therapist considers whether an upbeat closure is necessary, an even flow continued, or an additional activity is required to contain aroused feelings. Closure cannot be planned carefully ahead of time as it is the actual outcome of all that has gone before.

The therapist gauges the opportune time to announce that it is nearing the time to end. This may be after 20 minutes, 40 minutes, or an hour of group development. A familiar group is asked for their suggestions as to how to complete the session. When group members are not vocal or verbal, holding hands, an activity not always possible at the beginning of the group, may be the result of the input from the session. This kind of accomplishment can be tried with any item or movement introduced at the first part of the session with which members found some difficulty. Introduce the item again and observe how more members perform with greater success. In addition, repeating the activity used to open the group for closing is appropriate. For example, if "hello" was said in French, Spanish, sign language, a game or a handshake, use the same means to say "goodbye." The day and date may be reviewed and an announcement made of the next time the group is to meet. Reminders of things to practice or think about can be included. In addition, one of the following may be chosen from the appropriate category listed below.

Use Upbeat Activities With Group When Members Appear Too Subdued:

- Stamping down on paper cups;
- Conduct a short, fast circular movement with all members together;
- Hold hands and raise them up, shake, squeeze, and lower;
- Sing a goodbye song, clap along;
- Pass around beverage.

Use Routine Activities to Maintain Prevailing Mood With Group Members:

- Repeat the opening activity;
- Repeat a routine, such as affirmations;
- Pass a good touch, eg, a touch to the shoulder, knee, elbow, and cheek or head as is appropriate for the particular group;
- Group members can lean forward and playfully pile their hands on top of each other, pulling away one hand at a time;
- Depending on appropriateness, group members may hold elbows in a circle, then move closer together to place arms around the shoulders or waist of the persons side them, and then pile hands on top of each others' hands, pulling away one at a time.

Use Relaxing Activities When Group Ends With High Spirits:

- Serve a snack or beverage;
- While standing, close eyes and hold hands all together for as long as it is necessary to calm group. A group member then announces when it should end;
- Group members can say a prayer, a poem, repeat names, or what they are going to do after the session;
- Allow for some lingering time to occur.

Your Own Suggestions Below:

CHAPTER 6

Integration of the Five-Stage Mechanics

The mechanics of the Five-Stage group have been described thus far. A way of looking at attitude, a brief examination of group process, reminder of the specific analysis of sensory inputs that is part of Five-Stages, and some of the functional outcomes to be observed when using the Five-Stages are now discussed.

Group Process

When conducting the Five-Stage group, two fundamental beliefs must exist in the therapist's mind: One is that each participant can learn and that some wisdom exists within each group member that needs to be shared. Even though the group is composed of people who find it difficult to express their needs in an organized manner; even when they are enslaved to emotions that they cannot effectively harness to act on their environment, they know something others do not know. This is true even with members who are not sure of their rights or roles, what questions to ask, how to assess a situation, or how to balance the scales of their outer powerlessness with their inner power. This is true even when they do not know exactly how to physically comfort and activate themselves. They have experience and possess a wisdom that they can share and, in turn, receive from the other members. In the sharing of that wisdom, something happens to everyone. Some wisdom, even in a less than satisfactory group, is imparted to someone in the group just as the sun shining affects some growing element on that day. It is the sharing of this wisdom, starting with the therapist, that must be encouraged to happen throughout the session. It usually takes its form through some kind of relating to self, others, and objects. (Ross, pgs. 13-37, 1987)

Thus, considering the process in the group is just as important as in any kind of therapeutic group. However, traditional methods must be altered in responding to group dynamics when considering the nature of the population and the introduction of activities. In the Five-Stage structure:

- Using very brief, general discussions of here and now occurrences;
- Promoting successful motor outcomes in participants, as moving competently is another way of expressing good feelings;
- Using touch/tactile tracts, the therapist simultaneously touches and smiles with verbal direction and encouragement in an important, primary interpersonal interaction.
- Modeling by therapist, who also can explain why an activity is chosen;
- Providing frequent praise and positive affirmations;
- Supporting the practice on each member's part to *contribute*, to *lead*, and to be *nurtured* by the group;
- Observing to the group how the latter was done by members; and
- By encouraging group members to develop responding to each other,
  are some of the fundamental means for attending relevantly to group process in the Five-Stage Group. (Ross, 1987) These means are used in the newly formed group to convey acceptance. When a group becomes closely knit and familiar, acceptance is not synonymous with complete approval as destructive behaviors cannot change in this way. Sometimes, the therapist can describe what she sees, how it affects her in the group, and what she wants to see without attacking or blaming. However, this is incredibly difficult. When conducting the Five-Stage group with the special populations addressed in this book, the therapist is obliged to reflect at length before taking action. Several sessions of waiting for just the right time often makes a successful endeavor, and therapists should not feel that they have missed an opportunity when they have not attended to destructive behaviors immediately. It must be done with considerable thought, simplicity, and briefness, and differs greatly in degree from the way it may be handled in other verbal and activity groups. Attending effectively to destructive behaviors is possible only in an ongoing, very familiar group where considerable trust exists.

Analyzing Activity From a Neuroscience Base

Action and activity is addressed from a physiological viewpoint as much as possible. It is an important part of the task analysis of every action and activity presented in the group. For example, the simple act of group members holding hands is a symbolic and psychological act that provides unity and physical contact to the group. In addition, the therapist recognizes that tactile, proprioceptive, and temperature inputs are being presented. Some may become aware of a sweaty palm or a cold hand, resulting in behaviors that require discussion so that members may examine their choices. The group can be asked to respond or the suggestion can be made that holding the wrist is all right. It may underlie the rejection of a peer, which is sometimes best handled by silent waiting and no action by therapist so that members must resolve it. As hands hold and swing, some traction is provided to the shoulder girdle facilitating the neuromuscular message to tight shoulder muscles to relax, as well as to move with increased ease. This familiar, positive, and little act accomplishes much. When activities are seen as not only providing a motor or an emotional outcome, but also a broad combination of a total affect, it is then that the therapist begins to appreciate the hitherto unnoticed properties of simple movements and the changes they can affect. Group members making eye contact, passing a weight, looking at a picture, or the therapist moving around the group or physically guiding a participant must be seen as an integrated whole. It is a total process, gearing everyone to maintain postures, interest, focus, and, finally, performance through physiological facilitation because the right amounts of sensory, social, and emotional inputs at the right time are assisting the electrochemical firing needed for the adaptive response. These inputs cannot be skipped over lightly, dismissing them as one might with populations other than those addressed here. Other populations have capacities to over ride unpleasant little sensations but special populations only may grow to do so in a group of long-term duration if they continue to come to the group. When cohesiveness falls apart and means are used to reassemble, such as the therapist whispering, using a verbal statement, introducing a weight, novelty, or central item for all to hold on to and this brings temporary attention, this is not a mystery. All the structures of the central nervous system relating to attention on a reflexive level are being stimulated. Applying the neurosciences and observing the outcome of every aspect offered in the group contributes to better results with special populations with more predictive outcomes in mood and behavior, and movement and performance. Chapter 7, the relevance of theoretical treatment, approaches addresses this in greater detail.

Suggested List of Demonstrated Behaviors and Performances Observed From Using Action and Activities

This list is not inclusive. It also is arbitrary in its selection of items grouped under headings as some items can fit under more than one heading. The list contains only positive behaviors that may accrue as a result of work done within the group session. Any one, or a few combinations, of the functional behaviors can be used as the group objective for a day's session. Documentation then reports on the degree of limitation, skill, and performance observed in individual members with regard to the selected functional behaviors during a particular session.

Functional Motor Behaviors Demonstrated

- Acts alerted, movement facilitated;
- Acts relaxed, calm, controlled movement;
- Displays bilateral coordination, eye hand coordination, fine motor;
- Improved muscle tone, strength, range, endurance noted;
- Maintains balance, displays postural flexibility;
- Demonstrates a degree of ability to plan motor activity and to isolate parts of body.

Functional Cognitive Behaviors Demonstrated

- Exhibits the components of attention, eg, detect, select, sustain or persist, shift, and track or recall (Toglia, 1989);
- Paraphrases information;
- Displays initiative, imagination;
- Understands abstract ideas, displays humor;
- Exhibits memory for immediate, recent, or long-term recall;
- Displays judgment, problem solving, decision making;
- Accepts and makes use of teaching strategies to plan and organize.

Functional Emotional/Interpersonal Behaviors Demonstrated

- Participates in some or all of the stages;
- Demonstrates interpersonal skills, such as sharing and interacting;
- Displays alert, aware behavior in the use of space;
- Exhibits self-control and tolerance for others;
- Exhibits assertiveness;
- Expresses enjoyment and satisfaction;
- Expresses feelings;
- Cooperates, competes, compromises appropriately;
- Accepts leadership role;
- Displays risk taking.

Relevance of Sensory Integration and Other Theoretical Treatment Approaches to the Five-Stage Group

"Sensory integration theory is broader in its use than just sensory integration treatment." (SII, 1988, page 11)

"The Bobaths have traditionally worked with cerebral palsied and developmentally delayed children, but other people have expanded the Bobath's concept of posture and mobility to include additional disabilities." (Adler, 1983, page 1)

"A person uses all the performance components skills - motor skills, sensory integration, visual perception, cognition, psychological components, and social interaction -to perceive the environment." (Abreu and Toglia, 1987, page 439)

Introduction

Conducting a group appears to be psychological, dealing only with thought and words. Yet, for our special populations, the physiological aspect must receive serious consideration. It is through the ability to understand and influence physiological response that we chiefly have an affect on the individuals in our groups. Movement produces immediate and profound physiological changes that can influence behavior.

"The ability to move is dependent upon many factors. These include intact neuromusculoskeletal systems, central motor systems, perceptual integrity, sensory registration and integration, motor planning, cognition, drive, emotion and environment....Regardless of a therapist's area of practice, the evaluation of a client's ability to move and adapt to the environment is central to that practice." (DiJoseph, 1984)

Through using the group approach, this chapter suggests the means by which the physiological responses to movement and, indeed, to all group events, may be understood for the purpose of improving treatment.

It is not within the province of this book to explain those physiological responses in a comprehensive manner, but rather to show how application to practice was derived from the selected theory.

For example, following the introductory stage in a session with a geriatric population, attractive, bright, red barbells are selected for movement and handed to group members. With our special populations, there is often little we can do to know what is going on inside the individual. Asking for the information may not disclose it. By providing in this context a physical object, such as the barbell, there will be an observable response that is apt to reflect operating conditions in each individual. A refusal or acceptance is accompanied by change in motor behavior. Limbs adjust to the weight and surprise is seen on the face, in addition to other emotions aroused by the surprise, color of the item, and novelty of the situation. Rejection may take place, and we learn something about the individual from how that is experienced, which may suggest an alternate approach for more positive results next time. Perhaps it is too novel or too soon for the group and we must attend to that. (Allen, 1985, Chapter 7 and Ross, 1987, Chapter 6). Or, acceptance and some exploration of the object by group members may take place, and we can learn the degree to which each one can incorporate and use something new. Our special group member rarely comes to us prepared to bring up problems, but he can be roused to demonstrate them through the media of physical props and contacts.

The initial physiological responses reveal the psychological aspect of behavior with which the therapist may interact. With this particular group, there was a consistent rejection of the barbells. I could offer the barbells from time to time and use this slightly irritating means to gain attention. Changing the item as I verbalized my willingness to do so increased cooperation. Although they were a low-functioning group, I learned they still could make choices and be consistent in their likes and dislikes.

The psychological and physiological aspects of response are intertwined in the science of brain and behavior. As therapists with special populations, from what sources may we gain more understanding of the physiological basis of human responses to stimuli? What objects, movements, kinds of physical touch, and kinds of physical arrangements should be selected to facilitate the most relevant and adaptive responses?

It is necessary to unite the social sciences equally with the physical sciences concerning behavior if we are to work competently with our special populations. Therapists in psychiatry endow therapists in physical disabilities with a special mystique and vice versa. With our special populations, the luxury of such separation is not possible. This is not alarming or new, just reluctance in practice to accept the oneness that exists.

A review of the central nervous system (CNS) either in self-study or at a workshop can help. The more that is known about reception, retrieval, integration, interpretation, and response as processed by the CNS, the better knowledge the therapist has for selecting and presenting the appropriate objects, movements, and activities to our special populations to facilitate the most relevant and adaptive responses.

The Role of Sensory Integration in Motor Rehabilitation

One way of learning about the CNS is to gain
an understanding of sensory integration theory and principles.

Sensory integration (SI) is a "neurophysiological process by which sensory information is organized and interpreted" and "principles of sensory integration are applicable to all central nervous system dysfunction." (Selherzahn, as cited in Scardina, p.4) SI theory focuses on specific structures within the CNS and this can organize an approach toward conceptualizing the CNS. This approach does not minimize any part of the CNS, but provides an important guide for seeing relationships between the development of sensory centers such as the vestibular, proprioceptive, and tactile systems that lay the foundations for change and growth. When these centers develop normally, they promote the acquisition of physical skills for motor performance. These physical skills (Table A) underlie the competence and mastery required by all human beings as they grow toward independence and responsibility in directing their lives.

When the essential neural pathways of the initial sensory centers do not develop in a timely fashion in the child, according to SI theory failure to process external information adequately may occur. Such SI dysfunction may cause the child to appear clumsy, sloppy, and display a disorganized approach in action or avoid opportunities to learn, change, develop through action. (SII,

1988) Such an individual may look quite active without accomplishing very much. SI therapy provides specific kinds of movement and physical contact that is expected to establish the needed neural connections.

Some portion of the special populations we serve may have been untreated children, but others may incur which resemble SI dysfunction. Through trauma, disease, or sensory deprivation (Corcoran, 1987; Ayres, 1972, pg. 21) some of the stability of earlier established sensory centers may be lost. As we gain an understanding of the CNS structures involved, we learn how they regulate and influence each other by means of special kinds of *stimulation*. This stimulation cannot be offered indiscriminately.

Sensory integration provides an understanding
of how movement helps organize behavior.

Movement fires receptors to the brain and stimulates senses, which help integration and organization.

SI therapy uses movement as its therapy. Movement also is employed in the Five-Stage group approach. Therefore, understanding how movement may help to organize behavior theoretically can serve to guide what kind of movement, when, and how movement can be helpful in the group. Using the principles of SI does not infer providing specific SI therapy. The five stages provide sensorimotor, perceptual, and cognitive activities in a systematic way to remediate disorganized behavior or disabling conditions that may or may not be the result of SI dysfunction. In this manner, SI principles regarding movement and understanding of response are being applied and carefully observed by the results the therapist sees. Regardless of cause, it is the same nervous system for all persons that responds to stimulation. SI principles describe uses and limitations of activities for stimulation. This implies that all activities are analyzed before being presented so that a systematic enhancement of the CNS may be achieved. This enhancement is another way of looking at integration, which is achieved through the selection of sequential movement activities provided throughout the Five-Stage group session. The subsequent paragraphs describe how enhancement may occur within the Five-Stages.

Sensory integration theory particularly illuminates
the use of proprioceptive input in movement.

"Proprioceptive input tells the brain when and how the muscles are contracting or stretching, and when and how the joints are bending, extending, or being pulled or compressed. This information enables the brain to know where each part of the body is and how it is moving." (Ayres, 1979) Ayres addressed proprioception together with the vestibular and tactile sensory input in treatment for the learning disabled child. SI theory hypothesizes that the child lacks these inputs and these neural pathways are inadequately developed. Following a standardized assessment and diagnosis, the appropriate amount of input with the use of special equipment on an individual basis is prescribed to be carried out in SI therapy

Some prescribed treatment in therapy consists of having the child wrapped in a rug and rolled, or having the child climb inside a tire tube and swung. Other suspended equipment is used with the child that provides much vestibular stimulation in addition to proprioception. With this total body pressure and compression, the child is getting the kind of information he needs to feel more comfortable and, ultimately, to process his behavior in a more positive manner. The need to feel more aware of one's self for a greater sense of physical and emotional security can be a need for anyone regardless of age or cause. The cause of the agitation and great distractibility observed in members of special populations is often unknown to us but tends to mimic the hyperactive or distractible child who seems to benefit from SI therapy. It is difficult to offer the total body pressure described for the child to a group of adults but we can offer other means for proprioceptive input. Then, we can observe what change occurs and how consistently this happens with similar input. Therefore, the concept of proprioceptive stimulation for groups must become a part of the therapist's repertoire. There may be a need to construct a different underlying hypothesis for what we see from that which SI theory considers; however, let us not hold up the works while doing this.

In groups when members demonstrate agitation, apathy or confusion, *proprioceptive input is the sensory input of choice*. It can be applied by the therapist as she uses a vibrator or firmly grasps the hand and the arm of the group member. The therapist can lean into the shoulders from the back or front of the individual, provide a bear hug as appropriate, stand in the center and throw a bean bag to each member, or move with each member forcefully using the item distributed for movement. Turning a twisted sheet made to look like a jump rope between two members, and then assisting in getting it to move along the diameter of the circle of members, provides proprioception. Group members may be assisted in providing their own proprioceptive input as they use the vibrator, reach for and rub on hand lotion (on arms and legs, too), and apply perfume or aftershave. They may be instructed to push or lean into hands, massage themselves, clap vigorously, stamp or jump on paper cups, and move about with weighted objects. Activities are invented with these actions in mind. Tactile stimulation as well as some vestibular stimulation is included as it would be impossible to do otherwise. A more in-depth description of tactile stimulation to invite adaptive responses is discussed in "Group Process." (Ross, 1987)

The group may collectively provide proprioceptive stimulation when holding hands and shaking them, or having to shift to pass weights or weighted objects. Members must hold and examine them first, aiding in focus and reducing distractibility. Such objects might be a heavy framed hand mirror, a weighted candle (it can be textured, too, or smell strongly for arousal), and any solid iron object, such as a sculpture, candleholder, or antique item, can be examined. Bean bags can be thrown to each other or used to bounce on a parachute or on one's toes. A heavy bowling ball to roll or kick, or a resistive object to punch provides proprioception. The therapist must put meaning into this and introduce the activity judiciously. Given the usual circumstances, applying a number of these activities, one right after the other, will bring about a calm alertness in populations that may be immobilized and unable to initiate their own organized behavior.

The therapist cannot plunge into these activities but may, using the stages, proceed in an orderly, systematic manner with the therapist first providing the proprioceptive and tactile input individually. Go back and forth between having the group doing this collectively and having the individual handling his own input. This is what planning a group and gaining experience and skill is all about. Depending on activities selected, and with such an accumulative procedure, agitated or apathetic group members usually are ready to attend to the tasks of Stages III or IV. Proprioceptive input undoubtedly is a powerful tool.

Movement may help to organize behavior;
it also can serve to disorganize.
SI principles emphasize the significant influence of
sensory experience upon the nervous system.

There is optimal performance with the correct amount of stimuli which, if overdone or indiscriminately used, overarouses and disorganizes the individual. Therapists must discern this when it happens. It was exactly this phenomenon that created the basis for the five stages. As I first began to work with groups of overlooked patients on hospital wards, I thought that I wanted to obtain any response. When at the end of a session, as I gathered up my equipment, hands banged on trays, feet were extended so others might trip, foul or loud words were being heard, fighting occurred, or medication was refused, as well as at times, there was loss of bowel or bladder control, I realized I was not looking for these outcomes. I felt I must take responsibility for these outcomes when a majority of group members consistently displayed any one of these following a group.

I reasoned that patients had oriented to and registered the activities presented as they had attended and participated to the extent possible. Gradually I came to see that the activities were not the issue, but that the order and the manner of presentation made a difference. I made changes and observed the results. I was lucky in that I had a controlled, captive audience in the mid-70's. Discharges were very few, innovations few, and I was the only change agent in the back wards of a large state psychiatric hospital treating neurologically involved, psychiatric, mostly geriatric, long-term patients.

Each session I began to take time to make everyone feel very much recognized. Hence the orientation stage. Since interests and skills varied, I reasoned that I needed a variety of activities to appeal to those who did not like one thing but might engage in another. Hence the different stages emerged. That was not the only reason for the differing stages. In "Group Process" (Ross, 1987), additional rationale is offered for the specific ordering of the stages. It is sufficient to add that I noted that very short activities with considerable watching, waiting, and passing slowed down any escalation of unwanted excitement at the beginning. This can be accomplished by using objects to be passed around that are reactive in some quick way, such as when held, squeezed, or turned, emits unexpected air, sound, or change of shape. Hundreds are on the market and need to be accumulated. To end such a group, it would be necessary to introduce quieting activities so that the created energy could be used by group members to internalize the good feelings they had acquired. I had observed that if participants left a group on too high a note, this often resulted in restless, maladaptive behavior following the group. Hence the order of the stages occurred. In between the beginning and the end of the session, activities need more time and thought as to how to be presented so that the accumulative sensory inputs achieve the desired physical and behavioral goals for the group. Therefore, activities require a *special sequence* for their introduction with special thought given to presentation. To start with a simple action to collect everyone must be a rule. The task analysis must consider not only the physical aspects but the range of emotional responses inherent in the task. It is up to the therapist to take full responsibility for the sensory stimulation she is providing, watching, and modifying to prevent the occurrence of disorganization.

The therapist cannot take responsibility for the screamer, wanderer, or other unpredictable individual who is being tried out in the group, initially, for possible benefits. These persons can create havoc but with skill and patience may be included and could stay for a short period in the group. To continue persistently with such individuals must be up to the therapist to decide. The group alone cannot responsibly handle a person whose situation may require a review of medication, change in environmental circumstances, or the need for other disciplines to become involved.

The group cannot respond adequately to whatever the therapist brings when confusion abounds in the environment of the group. This occurs with insufficient or inappropriate space being provided for the group such as where visitors come and go or nurses, doctors, maintenance workers, or others may interrupt the session. The miracle of our group intervention stops here. If it is a very short interruption, I incorporate it into the group by inviting group members to tell me what I should do about it or how they feel about it. One day an aide brought her primary care patients (three members out of eight sitting in the group) ice cream. No one seemed to care until I made it an issue for this passive group in a long-term care facility to examine and resolve. They all suffered from severe memory loss, but feelings of being left out appear not to diminish even when memory does. If the interruptions are too great to overlook, I must quickly end the session. Recognizing the impact of these occurrences is important so that such conditions are reported and prevented from happening frequently.

Sensory integration provides a concept for selecting activities that promote calming and alerting responses in sensory centers.

Although specific sensory systems receive focus in SI theory and treatment, it is unlikely that only one system ever is used alone. Systems are used in combinations. SI has recognized the impact of such sensory systems as proprioception, vestibular, and tactile systems that, when excited or inhibited, influence the CNS in its response as well as promote maturation of the nervous system. The use of these systems to stimulate the CNS to inhibit or excite behavioral responses can be generalized to all sensory centers. Appendix B, Items 1 and 2, suggest some ways to think about alerting and calming many of the sensory centers to influence behavioral and motor responses.

A premise of SI theory is: "Treatment which provides controlled sensory input, within the context of meaningful activity, and which results in an adaptive response (or behavior) will enhance sensory integration and improve behaviors." (SII, 1988, pg. 6) The stages imply a plan to use selected meaningful activity that will be acceptable to our special populations. The quality of the participation can be observed for the adaptive response (or behavior). The results may not be long-lived, nor did SI theorists mean it to occur immediately as a consequence of sensory stimuli, but that more calm and alert behavior is exhibited. In groups where membership remains fairly unaltered over a long period, good changes are observed by this writer. Is it taking a giant leap to suppose that in some way, brain processing in group members is better

Table 7-A
Sensory Integration Development

Stage I	Stage II	Stage III	Stages, IV, V
The inherent function of the nervous system and information from the senses of	Are used to develop	The sensorimotor abilities to learn more concrete concepts and to develop	Use of these abilities develops an automatic level of function in
Touch	Body Scheme	Eye-hand coordination	Reading
Movement	Reflex maturation	Ocular motor control	Writing
Gravity	Center of gravity awareness	Postural adjustments	Spelling
Vision	Motor planning ability	Auditory-language skills	Number work
Hearing	Postural balance	Visual-spatial perception	Problem solving
Smell	Awareness of two sides of the body	Emotional stability	Sequencing
Pain	Balance between the protective and discriminative sensory systems	Mastery of environment	Ability to conceptualize
Temperature		Feelings of adequacy	Independent work
		Behavioral control	Spontaneous play
			Creativity
			Ability to form meaningful personal relationships

Note: Column titles have been added to indicate how the Five-Stage approach discussed in this text coincides with Gilfoyle and Hays model.

Adapted from Gilfoyle, E.M. and Hays, M.A. 1980. *Totems,* Vol. 3, Rockville, MD: The American Occupational Therapy Association, Inc.

organized? The need to observe and report these changes must be a part of clinical practice as leaders in the field suggest. (Henderson, Advance, AJOT, 1988)

Sensory integration, among other developmental theories, suggests a sequential list of skills and tasks that is acquired chronologically and contribute to the next skill level.

A developmental approach is helpful as a guide. What we can learn about task accomplishment at certain ages (Ayres, 1979, Pg. 103), reflex development (Ayres, 1972, pg. 79), other developmental changes (Willard and Spackman, pg.690, 1983), and from Appendix E, can be supportive as well as suggestive of appropriate activities to select for special populations. Nolan (AJOT, 88) reports her research results to show that "the loss of functional abilities in late-stage dementias seem to occur in reverse order of their development in childhood." Allen suggest this, also. (Allen, Chap. 16, 1985) More research is required for other kinds of regressive states, such as is experienced with brain trauma or diseases, to know whether this is applicable outside of the dementias. It is worthwhile to know just how the aging process does proceed even when no disease is apparent. Planning in terms of what can or cannot be expected allows for appropriate goal setting and the design of more realistic programmed activities. These activities often are bogged down by dictums of age appropriateness without considering the individual. Whatever is pleasurable, meaningful, and not harmful in any way is advantageous to consider as activity for special populations. Programs must be individualized. The whole subject of the nature of regressive states predictably will receive more vigorous study in the next decade.

The progression of sensory integration development can be recapitulated in a group session.

Table A is a chart of sensory integration development. This chart displays four columns, the first of which lists the inclusion of many sensory centers, which is the way the five stages need to be viewed, namely, as arousing many sensations appropriately. This first column also may be compared with the first stage (orientation) where the message must be made abundantly clear that the individual member is welcomed and acknowledged by the special stimulation the therapist provides through as many of the senses as possible. The therapist signals this through touch, sound, facial expression, and supplies she brings so that each group member feels comfortable, safe, and wanted. The participant usually wants to attend when his interests and needs are met.

Although there are more sensory centers than are listed in the above chart, the principle behind this listing is to indicate that as centers develop normally, the skills in the second column can emerge. Eye movements synchronize with neck, head, limbs, and body movements through reflex integration and maturation. Body scheme is promoted. Adequate muscle tone activates postural balance to encourage motor planning, which heightens awareness of bilaterality. Not shown on this chart, but depicted in the Ayres' chart on SI development (Ayres, 1979, p. 60), is the bonding of the infant with mother through good touch and handling, which provides further security needed to motivate movement. This may correspond to the second stage in our groups. When using appropriate objects and with appropriate touch, the therapist encourages a sense of body awareness and scheme through challenging motor planning movements. Balance is preserved through stimulating equilibrium responses in movement, which contributes to increased awareness of body scheme. Furthermore, movements are designed to encourage bilaterality, which reinforces all of the above. (Ross, 1987) The therapist, like a good partner, must help, guide, touch, even bond appropriately to promote a balance between the protective (touch) and discriminative (tactile) sensory sensations.

As the child achieves a developing sense of where he is in space and how to use limbs and body to get what he wants, as well as sufficient attention span to go after what he wants, a sense of mastery, adequacy, and motivation evolves. At this time, general global skills begin to break up in every area of development. Theory speculates that lateralization of the hemispheres now occurs. The left hemisphere becomes specialized in speech and language, as well as the establishment of skill in the dominant hand, and the right hemisphere becomes specialized in spatial judgments and form recognition. This may be observed in the chart's third column. Returning to the five stages, tasks presented become more specialized and formalized as this third column is applied to Stage III. We use the emerging sparks of cohesiveness, the feelings of satisfaction with the way movement has energized, and the more focused attention in our group participants to help members accept more specific demands. Visual motor perceptual activities can be introduced with greater possibilities for achievement. Surprise and pleasure may be voiced. Much of this is observed in posture, facial expression and willingness to perform.

The fourth column may be viewed as outcomes. The changes that have taken place progressively have produced a child who has an automatic level of function in all the areas involving memory and learning. The individual will now spend the rest of his life perfecting the ensuing outcomes that we arbitrarily summarize to be such end products as independence, creativity, and satisfactory interpersonal interaction. At this time in the group, by the fourth stage, memories can be prodded with some success, awareness of others is present, and some additional risks may be taken by the therapist to encourage verbalization and interaction or even reintroduce an activity that was not successful at an earlier stage.

Dr. A. Jean Ayres, the originator of SI Theory, depicts five columns in her view of SI development, but the outcomes of development remain the same. (Ayres, 1979) For our purposes, and with our indulgence in the imaginative use of such tables, Stage V becomes the final time to reinforce unconditional acceptance and encouragement to sustain effort in a growth process. No new activities are introduced, just the will of the group at whatever level it can be discerned, is encouraged to surface.

Finding assistance in the use of SI principles and theory to work with our special populations does not make us SI therapists, just as using psychoanalytical terminology to explain the behaviors we see, or to interpret the group process we observe, does not make us psychoanalysts. But understanding SI theory and principles offers one of the most substantial theories for being as effective as possible with special populations. We now go on to examine other useful theories and principles as we are never finished with the business of reshaping our skills with fresh insights.

The Role of Neurodevelopmental Theory and Other Approaches in Motor Rehabilitation

No one approach can attend adequately to our multifaceted special populations. The mandate of the Five-Stage Group is to offer a variety of activities in such a way that participants always will find something to try because it will be irresistible. Knowing how to assess the needs of the individual, how to rearrange the task for success, and how to be flexible in changing plans to meet immediate unexpected events requires a background, in a number of approaches. In addition to understanding the CNS, learning about the neuromusculoskeletal system is important to the therapist's and relevant to the participant's performance in the five stages. Neurodevelopmental theory relating to the neuromusculoskeletal system has been developed.

Neurodevelopmental (NDT) theory and principles began in the 1940's with its introduction by Dr. Karol and Mrs. Berta Bobath. The latter, a physiotherapist, worked with cerebral palsied children and later continued her work to include patients who had suffered cerebral vascular accidents. In the concept of "Neuro-Developmental Treatment," Berta Bobath states, "The problem of children with cerebral palsy is seen as one abnormal coordination of muscle action, that is to say of abnormal patterning of muscle function with a poverty of motor patterns, rather than one of weakness or paralysis of muscles. Hence, in treatment emphasis is laid on inhibiting abnormal patterns of posture and movement and on facilitating the greatest possible variety of innate normal basic motor patterns, such as head and trunk righting, arm-hand support, rotation and equilibrium reactions." (Bobath, 1979)

NDT is more a concept than a series of techniques (Davis, Preface, 1985) (Bobath, 1975) (Eggers, 1987) (Banus, Pgs. 318-20, 1979) (Adler, 1983). Viewed in this way, NDT can contribute to the way in which we can help group members who display a reluctance to move, timid movement, postural asymmetry, or outright abnormal movement. Proper positioning, a key issue in NDT, will be emphasized, especially for geriatric members who come to us in gerichairs, low couch seats, and arm wing backs that hide their view. Transferring to a straight chair and upright positioning is required for a working session. Presenting activities in shifting, reaching, and bending hips and knees that stimulate balance responses, to prevent a collapse into flexion or extension and to work for adequate contraction for stability, will underlie movement used in Stage II. Starting, stopping, and holding patterns necessary for function can be practiced in movement. Learning key points of control to influence tone and activity in parts of the body can be understood and used in assisting group members in movement.

NDT is a way of looking at movement difficulties.

NDT principles can provide an understanding of movement for function that is different from that of dance, aerobics, or exercise. These latter aspects should not be neglected, and therapists can enjoy and apply all the experiences that can be gathered to enhance group activities. Dance, aerobics, and exercise contribute to strength, endurance, and a sense of rhythm and expression, but executing a repetitive step does not mean generalizing it to function. NDT provides an understanding of normal movement versus abnormal patterns of movement. It prepares the therapist to be able to view performance and understand what may be preventing normal patterns. In special populations, abnormal movement patterns limit movement. Poor posture, inadequate balance, or problems in contraction exist because these are an integral part of their problems, regardless of causes.

Understanding NDT principles of movement patterns will suggest movement emphasizing segmentation of body parts, stabilization with shifting, elongation, and rotation, always observing for symmetry, variety, and quality in movement rather than trying to achieve the goals sought in exercise. An example of this was seen when working with some young adults with mild to moderate retardation. They demonstrated good dance and aerobic movements from some of the programs offered in their group homes or school. When I asked them to walk on top of 4-inch wide blocks raised one inch from the floor, they could not do this adequately. Nor could they walk rapidly backwards, or reach forward with their hands extending a plate toward the center of the circle without losing some balance. These latter skills are required to step over a puddle or other debris. These skills are required to reach for work in the work shop or to quickly get out of the way of an oncoming object. NDT addresses lags in normal motor development, such as in brain damage at birth and those problems that occur in disease or trauma like a cerebral vascular accident. We are not intending to do NDT treatment per se in our groups because that is best done one to one. But we can use treatment principles as a point of view for designing movement for functional needs and evaluating the process of performance other than is used for expression, endurance, and strengthening, although these are excellent secondary goals.

The items for use in movement in Stage II can be props for staging activities of daily living (ADL) and functional kinds of movements. Referring again to the plates described above, these were distributed to a group of elders who reside in a long-term care facility and require total care supervision. First we used the plates slowly flexing and extending fingers, wrist, and forearm in movement. Once we got into it, we began to pat ourselves with the plates on the small of the back, sweep the air, pick up from the floor, and reach body parts keeping in mind good positioning and proper stabilization for maintaining balance. These are the functional movements required to brush one's hair on the back of the head, pull up a zipper, fix a collar, put on a sweater, and don a shoe. These elders demonstrated enough flexibility and enjoyment while moving this way. NDT principles may be employed in all ADL activity. These principles serve as a stimulus for the design of movement combining it with function.

Learn about yourself and others from analyzing
postures as you and others move from lying, to kneeling,
to sitting, to standing and to walking.

While taking any experiential course or workshop, such as NDT, the learner becomes more aware of herself. You are lying down, kneeling, coming to standing differently from others; also, you are observing the postures of others as they perform in the workshop. You assist others and learn how to facilitate instead. You are learning to critique, take risks, and be vulnerable. In a dimension other than verbal, you learn about how you feel free or fearful, flexible or tight, inhibited or fluid in your own movements. You learn about your coping style, avoidance or acceptance of emotional pain, and appreciate how you go from stress to mastery. Knowing yourself better will be a great asset in acquiring a closer bond with special populations. They already have gone through this stress and need the special understanding fortified by the facilitation skills that you have acquired, so that you can help their mastery to emerge.

Neurodevelopmental treatment gives "permission" to handle or guide.

Most importantly, whereas some therapeutic approaches are provided by exposing the individual with dysfunction to equipment or talking them through an intervention, NDT expects the therapist, in the role of facilitator, to handle and guide the individual appropriately through movement. With our special population, touching by request and with knowledge is an important way to deliver intervention.

There are other neurodevelopmental approaches to movement that also expand the knowledge base for the Five-Stage group, combining the need to understand the central nervous and neuromusculoskeletal systems.

As examples, the theory base of Spatiotemporal Adaptation (Gilfoyle, Grady, Moore, 1989) and the Proprioceptive Neuromuscular Facilitation (Voss, 1972) provide excellent material to study as aids for further revelation of the powerful aspect of movement in human development, growth, and functioning. The Five-Stage group requires a well-seasoned approach that draws from a large pool of theories and principles to meet the diversity in special populations. It is a synthesis of the individual therapist's thought. The group is not a substitute for in-depth one-to-one therapy, but another way of meeting a broad spectrum of needs for a severely debilitated population.

An introduction into a new approach in therapy is refreshing and provides again the need to rethink old ways. Such therapies as the Feldenkrais Method, Myofascial Release, and the Cranio-Sacral approach, as well as others presently addressed (Advance, 1988), have important contributions and insights to make the group work, even if one just observes the leader's techniques used to teach her theories. Although each one has its special message, the underlying theme is to use touch, movement, and mental imagery efficaciously to decrease bodily tension, mental stress, and physical pain. The therapist has much to gain from her own relaxation and much more to offer our special populations in contemplating and exploring what can be adapted to group needs. The blossoming of so much thought, written material, and unique claims of success by each master theorist serves to reinforce the conviction that the most important common denominator in each one's success is the therapist's style, the degree of the therapist's conviction to serve and willingness to bond with the individual she is treating.

For group purposes, it is basically the attitude of the therapist toward movement that is important: Movement is for function and to facilitate functioning; to be able to see where the patient is "stuck," why he cannot help himself, and to be able to use a background of concepts to help make his movements more free in the environment.

Application of the Cognitive Rehabilitation Model to the Five-Stage Group

Reference so far has been made to differing but relevant therapies that are rooted in a neurophysiological base. Much has been happening in the perceptual-cognitive sphere since the inception of the Five-Stage group that may serve us in Stages III and IV. In the latter stages we want to accomplish in our groups what other groups set out to do but may not first prepare the group participant to receive or achieve. The group participant is prepared because of the firm conviction that this approach best serves the needs of special populations. We want to have a receptive and interested group as is realistic so that working on tasks that require concentration, organization, and self-control may be presented. Tasks presented in these stages may be considered in the realm of cognitive remediation.

The works of Allen and Toglia and Abreu are selected as examples for discussion because their therapies use a sensorimotor base. They do not emphasize verbal techniques. Also, both approaches differ radically in their assumptions of treatment and it is my belief that there are many similarities between the two populations that they treat. Both authors exemplify a cognitive approach to treatment.

Allen defines a cognitive disability as "a restriction in voluntary motor action originating in the physical or chemical structures of the brain and producing observable limitations in routine task behavior....The deficit is in the mental processes that usually guide motor actions. Just as a therapist measures range of motion to evaluate physical disability, he or she can assess cognitive level to evaluate impairments in thinking." (Allen, 1985, pg. 31)

She shares the conviction that there are not two major areas of practice—psychiatry and physical disabilities—but one. "Because psychiatric diseases are looking more and more like "regular" medical diseases, a prediction was made that future psychiatric occupational therapy practice would probably need to resemble physical disability practice." (Allen, 1988, Focus) This belief is promoted and is the tenor throughout this book.

Allen initially based her work of assessing cognitive level on the sensorimotor intelligence theory of Piaget. Impairments in thinking were and remain evaluated as observed in the patient's performance of a voluntary motor action such as required by a specific activity. However, continuing to develop her thoughts on the nature of therapeutic activity, what it is and what it is not, she became more influenced by Soviet psychological thought, which she felt is, "the only social science discipline using the concept of activity as a focus of study." (Allen, AJOT, 1987) Her writing is precise, singular, and invigorating as she reminds us by her example not to run along with a pack of unquestioned dogma or assumptions. The usefulness of her cognitive Level I will be discussed when addressing the issue of using criteria for choosing participants for the Five-Stage group. Her approach to using clinical observation of performance in various activities as a measurement of change is useful in the Five-Stage group. This report of clinical observation becomes an important service to other staff that the therapist can render in any facility. For example, working with a large population of low-functioning adults with mental retardation in a work services situation, I may see them once or twice a month in group. Therefore, my influence to create change is minimal. However, over a period of 2 to 3 years, I have noticed changes in behaviors emerging that were lacking at the time of their arrival into the program. Absolutely unable to perform initially, group members now frequently pass objects without a verbal or physical cue. They are able to imitate two to three postures in movement just by watching others. They sometimes pick up a dropped item when it is intended for them. They face towards the group and can hold hands on both sides simultaneously, although at times they still require a prompt. They accept new activities more readily.

When I reported this to staff they were pleased and could corroborate growth in these clients. Staff could take credit as a major influence for change. Caring supervisors at work and in living arrangements contribute to these developments. The occupational therapist is trained to know what attributes matter for growth in functional abilities and she contributes to reporting the behavioral changes noted, which provide a perspective for other staff. Allen's measurement of cognitive levels of functioning, descriptions of behaviors, of task analysis, and methods for using earlier and contemporary theorists to synthesize her own approach are some of the reasons for studying her work directly. Therefore, these relate indirectly to the stages but may sharpen observation of how group members perform in Stages III and IV.

The principles embodied in the Cognitive Rehabilitation Model proposed by Toglia and Abreu can enrich our skills as we conduct Stage III and IV. "Cognitive training involves systematic procedures designed to broaden the patient's capacity to process information and improve the client's ability to utilize efficient mental strategies. Perceptual Remediation or Cognitive Training is an approach shared by many health professionals working with the brain injured client. The approach's major assumption is that brain damage does not abolish the total ability to perform a task but reduces the ability to perform a task efficiently " (Toglia and Abreu, 1985).

Abreu and Toglia base their evaluation-intervention model on the theories of Alexander R. Luria, the late professor of Psychology at the University of Moscow, who was a major scholar and scientist in neuropsychology. "Our approach to treatment follows learning theory and behavior modification principles on an individual or group basis." (Abreu, 1985) In our groups, we practice cognitive skills through activities described by Abreu and Toglia as "orientation, insight, attention, memory, problem solving, and organization." (Abreu and Toglia, 1987) These therapists state that "Strategies to efficiently process information are not employed automatically. Clinically the patient may not automatically attend to the relevant feature of the task, group similar items together, formulate a plan, or break the task down into steps." (Abreu and Toglia, 1987) This applies to the need for the therapist to plan carefully the method of presentation and to think about the cues required by each individual participant to achieve success and reach for that learning experience.

We can learn the assists, cues, and adaptations group members require for success by observing individuals participating in the group. Abreu and Toglia state that "a portion of the occupational therapy cognitive-perceptual evaluation should emphasize quality more than quantity and function more than dysfunction." (1987) To ensure this, they recommend starting with test items that make minimal demands and to continue to increase the demand for processing information by the individual. Tests and activities ought not to be terminated following failure to understand standard or initial instructions. Watching how problem solving is addressed by the individual is necessary as it may provide insight for the therapist to conditions that promote performance or cause deterioration. Finally, watching how the same strategy used by an individual may work at times and not be useful at another may pose the need for more problem solving. How to reflect an accurate picture of the client's abilities and yet at the same time gain a more dynamic understanding of his needs in treatment is elaborated on in their work. This directly carries over to the way we might observe how group members perform. Are instructions too elaborate? Should we state all the steps of the activity, demonstrate it, have one member model it one step at a time, then repeat the steps verbally again, as we watch for what individuals may need in addition? I have tried many variations of this process before concluding what seems to bring the most likelihood of success for a particular group. Analyzing where performance breaks down and using the extensive knowledge these authors have helps provide solutions for better understanding of the strengths and weaknesses of special populations.

It is in the treatment design of "Cognitive Rehabilitation" where the study of the model of Toglia and Abreu can provide us with stimulation, useful strategies, and insights. Although their work is geared toward the traumatic brain injured, it is these principles that we need to use for our special populations who may or may not be categorized in this manner. These principles consider the nature of treatment and goals for treatment. Their treatment tools include the teaching/learning process, how it may be facilitated, and consideration of the uses of environment. The consideration of attentional deficits as presented in their workshops is very helpful in working with and understanding our special populations. Most importantly, these writers and clinicians remind us of the need for body alignment, positioning, and active movement required by the group member prior to initiating a treatment session with him. This also is an integral part of the structure of the Five-Stage Group, eg, Stage II addresses posture and movement prior to cognitive tasks. Study of their method can validate, suggest, and renew the therapist's attack on overcoming difficulties presented when working with special groups. Currently, these two therapists have separated to embark on individual endeavors of special interest so they will continue to make contributions to professional thought.

To summarize, there remains the never-ending and constant need to examine that which appears to us solid in its approach and pertinent to our needs in working with special populations. Good results in our groups are not accidents but an expression of our acquisition of skills through thought, study, and practice, both on the part of the therapist as well as the group member. This is reflected in our groups as individuals learn to feel safe, take risks, and work better together. They can often perform at the end of a session that which they were unable to do in the beginning of the session. Allen may view this as "reproducing," not learning. (Allen, pg. 383, 1985) Abreu and Toglia believe that brain-injured adults can be taught to facilitate their own learning. "The purpose of treatment using the cognitive rehabilitation model is to maximize existing potential by providing strategies to enhance the patient's ability to process and organize information efficiently." As therapists with special populations, we must work toward that goal using whatever theories, principles, and ideas other creative minds can contribute. It does not take long with our special populations to see what works.

The Need to Develop a Personal Approach

The underpinnings for all group endeavors may be considered like a triangle; each angle contingent on the other for the shape it is in. One angle may be marked "resources," the second angle may be marked "common sense" or "perspective," whereas the third angle is to be marked "humor." This chapter closes with a salute to humor. Robinson, (1977) was a forerunner of the many good books and articles now heralding humor in the health profession. In her writing, she demonstrated how humor can create a greater interest and persuade us to be more patient in our work. Humor sharply outlines vignettes occurring during the group session. For example, there is humor in the contrast of my seriousness or eagerness to work with the group versus the sometimes ludicrous environment embodied in a dirty, sticky floor, indifferent or sleeping participants, the lack of appropriate space in a large recreation hall, or the unwelcome interruption of someone who has come too clean the trays on the laps of some participants just as a tenuous attentiveness has been achieved. Humor must be tapped in our group members for the expansive feelings it arouses.

The following case example illustrates this. Working with a group of young adults who are mentally retarded, the Stage III task was to dig into a large paper bag, pull out an item, and describe or demonstrate its use. Some components of this exercise include form constancy, figure ground, possibly stereognosis, memory, body scheme, postural balance, bilateral motor coordination, crossing midline, and motor planning. One group member was a young man who was mute and usually displayed a "poker" face. "Bob" had been born in 1947 with Down syndrome. The following test scores placed him in the "profound range of mental retardation": Vineland Active Behavior Scale, 1985, social age - 2 years; Cattell Infant Intelligence Scale, 1984, mental age: 13 months; IQ: 2; Vineland Social Maturity Scale, 1985, social age: 2 years, 2 months; and language reception testing: 1 year, 10 months. Although initially appearing unaware, inattentive, unable to imitate postures, interrelate with peers, or accept touch from me during sessions, his group skills have developed in all the above areas over the past 3 years.

A chance group experience revealed cognitive and social levels that contrasted strangely with the above standardized scores. When requested to pull out something from the bottom of the very large paper bag, "Bob" withdrew a plastic, miniature derby hat. He deliberated and slowly put it on his head. He grinned and turned his head from one side to another to display it to the group. I was guilty of a moment of shock, which preceded my laughter. As the tiny hat sat upon his head, I felt very close to him as I shared his enjoyment. I saw new possibilities for experiences I would have the privilege to provide that could far exceed the expectations of standard psychological scores.

"Bob's" action reminded me to expect and encourage humor in group members. I would not want to miss the chance to learn this wisdom from him. Humor tops all theories and bonds everyone. It emblazons hope.

CHAPTER 8

Conducting the Five-Stage Group
Hello—My Name Is Mildred

"In the work that you do when you are being competent and, all the more so if you are being gifted, you are generating new knowledge. That generation of new knowledge occurs within the practice setting itself.....Practice, itself, is a generative activity." (Schon, 1988)

This chapter demonstrates how practice may produce knowledge for the therapist. Descriptions are included of some of the ways with which the Five-Stages, with emphasis on activities, have been applied to different kinds of special populations and what has been learned. Also, criteria for selecting group members will be suggested. In addition, every activity introduced by the therapist is subject to a task analysis. (Ross, 1987) However, presentation of the task is the only part of task analysis to be covered. Presentation always must consider the progressive gradations of every task from the simplest to the most complex and becomes a means by which the therapist discovers more knowledge about special populations and the tasks themselves. This chapter will provide examples of two different aspects of graded order in presenting tasks.

Examples of Presenting Tasks in a Graded Order

A puzzle that is constructed in about 10 minutes may be offered to group members in Stage III. The puzzle may be selected from the Appendices or an individually selected one containing a meaningful single subject in the foreground and having pieces that are easy to hold. Members can be regrouped from movement into a semicircle or placed at a table so all can view the action. A mobile population can work on the floor. Viewing the presentation from difficult, complex, and most challenging, to the easiest, most simple and least demanding, the following gradations of the same activity are considered by the therapist.

1) At the highest level, a picture of the puzzle, if it is on the box, is shown to group members. Then, the puzzle pieces are presented for the group to work on together.

2) An outline of the puzzle's perimeter can be constructed first by therapist. Then, pieces are distributed to members.

3) A completed puzzle is presented to group members. A number of pieces are removed totalling the number of group members. Each member awaits his or her turn to replace the piece.

4) The completed puzzle is shown to each group member and one piece is removed and given to the participant who is requested to put it back right away. When this is done successfully by the total group, then level 3 should be tried immediately following the success.

5) The completed puzzle is shown to each group member and one piece is removed and given to the participant who is requested to put it back right away. Hand over hand assistance should be provided to the member who requires this. Then therapist may suggest that the action be tried without assistance. When this can be done, then level 4 should be tried immediately following the success.

6) At the lowest level, matching of shapes may be considered first (see Appendix).

Another way of looking at presenting activity in a progressive, graded manner is to consider novel ways of presenting a familiar object with the emphasis on unexpected variations that challenge a person physically as well as his imagination. When doing this always start with the easiest request, eg, how to hold the article, regardless of the level of the group as this does not stifle anyone but rather organizes the whole group at once. The activity of passing a 3-lb. to 5-lb. weighted sandbag, which can have a special shape for attractiveness, is an example of this concept. The sandbag is not altered; but the differences in types of demands requested are unique and not necessarily more difficult or less difficult. Leading up to a novel use of the sandbag so that it will be used successfully becomes the reason to introduce gradually getting acquainted with the sandbag. Starting from the least novel and proceeding to the most novel, as experience has indicated, the sandbag is passed around in the circle from member to member. Then the therapist models, holding sandbag with both hands and moving her hands a little above and below her waist height, holding it close to the body. Participants, then, can imitate this. Therapist can try to toss the bag about 8 inches in the air and catch it. Each group member gets the same opportunity. Here, it can be noted, some activities lend themselves to both grading not only for novel ways but for complex ways. The therapist can balance the sandbag on her shoulder (to be followed by group members) and then on a raised knee or leg; and finally trying it on her head, which requires some good balancing adjustments for success. It is very important that precautions are exercised in selecting the appropriate population for this latter part of the activity. People with problems in the cervical area, with arthritis, or geriatric populations are not suitable for placing weights on the head although, working with weights up to the placement on the head may be appropriate. Decisions of amount of weight used must be thought out thoroughly by the appropriate personnel in charge. This may be the occupational therapist, the physical therapist, or the physician.

Grading the presentation of the task from simple to complex and from most familiar to most novel, as well as considering the initial orienting steps offered verbally and in demonstration by the therapist, starts the whole procedure properly. This is a truism, but it can be forgotten or poorly prepared. It marks the success or the failure of the reception of a presented task regardless of the merit of the task.

Criteria for Group Membership

The purpose for using the Five-Stage group approach is that it offers a method by which meaningful contact may be had with members of special populations, and permits a group to happen. Therefore, idealistically, all members of special populations should qualify. However, the word "group" is attached to the Five-Stages. There exists the condition of such regression or delay in development in some members of special populations that indicate a level where an appropriate response cannot be organized. This is well described by two authors and can be used as criteria for the Five-Stage group in selecting membership.

Use of the Parachek Geriatric Rating Scale (Parachek) and Treatment Manual (King, Lorna Jean, 1986) offer a quick, standardized screening of the geriatric population. Scores place the participant in one of three groups. Those persons whose test results placed them in Group I would not be included in the Five-Stage group. "Patients scoring in this range show sufficient impairments to require a substantial amount of nursing care. These patients respond better to short intermittent periods of attention over the waking hours than to long periods of sustained treatment." (Parachek and King, 1986) The full use of the Parachek Geriatric Scale and Treatment Manual can provide the basis for goal-oriented treatment plans, to include Group I patients. The latest edition includes abstracts of research projects from around the world that used sensorimotor activities with good results. (King, telephone communication, March 1989)

Another suggestion for means of selecting appropriate group membership can be gleaned from the very specific portrayal of the Level I patient described by Allen in the Allen Cognitive Levels assessment (Allen, 1985, pgs. 41-43). She writes,

> "Most sensory cues are ignored at level 1. Awareness of the external environment is restricted to a subliminal recognition of familiar cues. Attention is transient, slipping away unless commands are constantly repeated....The therapist's efforts to reach these people rarely meet with much success. They stare at a demonstrated action as if they do not see it. They do not clap their hands when the action is demonstrated, nor will they take an object when it is placed in their hands."

The Lower Cognitive Level Test (LCL) was designed by Allen to distinguish further between the first three levels of the Allen Cognitive Level Test (ACL). The Allen LCL is provided for the reader in a reprint from the complete description in Allen, 1985, and appears in an Appendix.

Therapists who are concerned that some member of a special population may be left out of a group because they appear inert and unresponsive due to acute medical problems or to sensory deprivation are urged to redo the Parachek scale from time to time. When no response is elicited to any changes provided by caregivers a "parallel response" group can be considered. (Parachek and King, 1986, pg. 36)

Application of the Five-Stages to Special Groups

Populations are similar, but no two groups in any of the special populations reported here can ever be identical or exactly reproduced by the reader. The reader as therapist creates and generates her own knowledge and learning in the doing of the group. What is valid here is the telling of one's own experience so that it can be added to and improved as it is recreated by others. However, one similarity found to be held in common by all members of all the groups described, which indicated use of the Five-Stage approach, was a problem with language. All of the participants have difficulty with expressive language *as a means of communication* as observed in their writing, verbalizations, or comprehension of language heard or read. They frequently misinterpreted, misunderstood, or did not hear or listen to what was said for a variety of reasons. With emphasis on activity and the belief that providing the selected activity in a sequential way heightened alertness, attentiveness, and recall, the

Five-Stage approach was used to overcome limitations with language and to enhance participation.

Four different populations will be described with an overview of their general characteristics. Objectives to be addressed by the group will be provided, followed by the description of a typical group.

The Group with Developmental Disabilities

When first applying the Five-Stage approach to special populations, treat yourself to adults with mental retardation. They will help you with their receptivity and naturalness to feel successful. However, the challenge of the severely, physically disabled, profoundly retarded young adult or young child is great, admittedly, but minute gains are usually greatly appreciated by other care providers that there is a good ripple effect for the great expenditure of effort. Both the profoundly and the moderately retarded and their groups will be described.

The Severely, Physically, Disabled, Profoundly Retarded Young Adult. Working one day with such a group of five older teenagers in a vocational setting, with hand over hand operations for the most part of the 2-hour period, I introduced a more social time together. Pulling two tables together, eight of us (including two caregivers) grouped around it so that help could be provided strategically. A battery operated robot with sparking antennas was placed on the table. He noisily went in one direction until touched and would then turn around and go in another direction. We became a group for the first time that morning as everyone focused on its movements. Just by resting arms on the table or getting up close to the table offered enough touch for the robot to come over and go away. Everyone got "touched" or could easily be helped to touch. One young girl always rose in zombie fashion when touched by another person and wandered away but, throughout this experience, remained seated. A blind young student could participate because he could hear the robot approaching and, despite severe spasticity, could extend his hand sufficiently for the robot to touch. We demonstrated the concept of "blocking" as against "pushing," further adding that if the robot was allowed to fall off the table, it would break and could not be used any more, so everyone was needed to cooperate in this game.

Another game tried was one in which the "Twister" cloth was placed on the table and each one was helped, sometimes hand over hand, to "slide" or "throw" a small bean bag to a given color. The spinner was used to decide the color so that two more actions could be learned. It became clear that our task would be to see how many different ways we could experience these four actions by using fun activities, as these are exactly some of the skills needed in a workshop. The fun of a game (Kielhofner and Miyake, 1981) was more motivating and produced more motor initiation than the little understood, piecemeal job each group member had to do earlier, no matter how carefully it had been explained. Furthermore, they became a group in the social sense of the word to a greater degree than just the work experience could provide.

It occurred to me that the entire morning with these students was an example of conducting an experience in Five-Stages. I always welcome them individually and warmly as in the first stage and explain the work project to them, which differs according to the work available in the workshop. The accomplishment of the assigned, sometimes paid for, task can be considered as Stage II. This task varied from visit to visit. It usually consisted of a great variety of packaging of craft supplies into organized units. Supplies come in bulk and must be reassembled, boxes must be constructed and later sealed, and packaging of items can be all assigned to the students. Sometimes a bulk supply of nails are to be put into 1 lb. boxes or paper must be torn for recycling. Stage III can address social needs for rewards of work through games like the two described above. In addition, selecting activities that *apply to grasping and proper placement of items or use of limb* in perceptual tasks promote growth in development for this level of student. The time then spent in eating lunch, toileting, cleanup and saying goodbye may be seen as Stages IV and V. The structure of the stages becomes useful to ensure that a comprehensive session in which essentials, such as greetings and leave takings with worthwhile sequential occurrences in between, are routine to provide a total experience where good change might occur. Behavior, taking risks to try something new, and attention span were all seen as improved in the workshop from that seen in their classroom in 70% of these students.

A Five-Stage group approach was attempted also with these same students when I visited in their classroom. Developmentally they may be considered from 1 to 3 years, too young for group skills to emerge or be expected. However, they have had some life experiences upon which the therapist may try to build. This becomes the rationale underlying a group format for these students. Whatever is gained in greater awareness of the environment, of each other and the self, makes the effort worthwhile. The Five-Stage group lasted about half an hour. The vibrator was used with wide and pleasurable receptivity, objects to move with to range limbs were attempted, much passing of different objects were provided for tactile and proprioceptive stimulation and to encourage contact with others in the group. Group cohesiveness did not appear to develop that could be sustained. However, purposeful behavior, cooperation, and attentiveness did improve moderately over the year in this group.

The 5-Stage Group with Adults with Moderate to Mild Mental Retardation.
A group format can address the list of needs for this special population. Their greatest requirements are to experience many activities and to do the same thing in many different ways. Sensorimotor objectives may be gross and fine

motor coordination and control to include the ability to isolate fingers; grade pressure of digits and hand grasp; and to use ipsilateral/alternate hand and foot movements in a variety of directions. Sensory integration components within this area may be to emphasize postural balance and gravitational security; visual motor integration; simple to complex experiences in motor planning, and to offer experiences in visual spatial performance. Attentional deficits may be addressed as well. Concepts such as focusing, stopping, starting, and continuing can be featured in activities. Other cognitive activities can highlight memory, expressiveness, following directions, initiating, and making decisions. Social needs usually can address relating appropriately to others such as cooperating, waiting for a turn, sharing, helping, and supporting. The concept of competing may have to be taught. The ease with which a therapist can find elements of all the above needs within so many activities and the enthusiasm usually found in this population makes this rewarding work. Progressive changes are certain to come with consistent treatment application. One hastens to add that not just one kind of treatment application will do it, but other environmental factors must be there, also. These are work and living arrangements that also are conducive to providing motivational factors for the individual to grow and make changes.

One group that has continued for more than 4 years, meets consistently once a week for an hour. Their ages range from the early 20s through the 50s. Only two members belonged to the original group, others have about 1 to 3 year's membership. Members leave the group because they are placed in supported employment situations in the community. Members are excused from their work in work services, formerly called a sheltered workshop, to come to the group. During the week they are sure to remind me of the next meeting and usually arrive on their own, unless they cannot remember which day of the week it is. Activities presently selected are to encourage continuing development of a movement repertoire, eye-hand coordination, and bilateral activities to improve motor planning, opportunity to practice initiative and memory, and to experience appropriate social interactions. Memory is an outstanding deficiency in mental retardation. Few are ever taught how to use cognitive learning skills to jog and assist poor memory, such as those used as treatment techniques with the traumatic brain injured. To learn and acquire knowledge, some degree of disciplined behavior is essential. With these formerly institutionalized individuals, disciplined behavior was never consistently practiced. Improvements have been noted when graded tasks are presented appropriately, when firm and encouraging insistence on trying is provided, and when time is taken to practice memory skills. Some excellent resources for understanding the needs of this population has been written by Lederman (1984), Herrick and Lowe (1984, 1988) and Hasselkus.

A recent group session consisted of all eight members. Members are considered in the moderate to moderate-mild range of retardation. Six require supervised living arrangements, which are presently group homes, and two live with their families. On this day, after greeting each other, the group was asked if they wished to work on initiative (explained as doing what had to be done without being asked) and leadership (taking responsibility that something would get done). The group was reminded that we always did certain kinds of activities and we did them in a certain order. So, what was it that we did first? They all knew that saying "hello" to each other was first and one member volunteered to greet each member. With one or two suggestive questions, they remembered that "exercise" was done next. Who wanted to lead the "exercise", decide on what to use, and whether there should be music? Ana volunteered, chose the large sand-filled soda bottles, and asked me which button on the cassette player to press for music. She raised her arms dramatically as if to conduct an orchestra, asked the group to look at her, waited some seconds, admonished one member to pay better attention, and proceeded to lead the group, non-stop, with the most unusual creativity in movement for about 5 minutes. Group members cheered and clapped for her. Ana has Down's syndrome and is excessively overweight. She is one who had most difficulty with flexibility and variety in movement when she joined the group in December 1983. Her present individual annual and quarterly objectives written prior to the group described above was that "Ana will intervene appropriately in group with newcomers, accepting guidance in this area," "Ana does not volunteer for a task she cannot perform during group sessions," and, "Ana will accept one activity that challenges balance, such as walking on top of a wide block or stepping from one hoola hoop ring into another without taking a step in between." Her leadership of the group gave her the needed opportunity to demonstrate progress toward goals.

I asked, "Following movement, what then do we do?" This required much memory prodding to elicit first some activities and, secondly, to classify these as different from exercise or movement. I suggested "thinking and acting," which I explained was different from movement where one could copy what others did without having to do it in a specific, definite way to succeed. Another group member, Marli, volunteered to lead this and picked out the dancing doll (World Wide Games) from a large stuffed locker closet. It was about one year ago when I had introduced it to this group and no one could use it successfully. At that time, we just took turns putting the doll in different positions on the paddle and naming those positions, ie, standing on its head, sitting with feet dangling, etc. Marli demonstrated quite well how to use it as it was meant to be used. She sat on top of a long paddle and held the doll motionless with her right hand, over the extended paddle while banging the paddle with her left hand causing the doll's loose wooden legs to tap out a rhythm to some jazz-like music. She had taken the doll out on her own to explore it once or twice before. Everyone appeared to have some success with this bilateral, fine motor, spatially oriented activity requiring more or less of

Marli's assistance. The very newest member who had never seen the doll needed much encouragement to keep trying, but Marli persisted, although he never quite mastered it at this session. Marli's individual goals in the group are to demonstrate appropriate behaviors toward peers and acceptance of self by displaying no pouting, impulse control, decision making, and persistence in tasks. She appears to have a good, yet untapped, potential. Interest and enjoyment appeared to be high as everyone waited to get their turn. When possible, group members learn best from each other.

"Now," I asked, "What do we do after we think and act?" Someone said that we can talk about how we feel about things. Another added then we say goodbye. So, for this group, the Five-Stages are discernable by "hello," "move," "think and act," "talk," and "goodbye." Realistically, it would take much more time and many more groups to integrate and generalize the learning that went on today. But, it was a heartwarming group having fun while demonstrating a desire to grow in self-discipline, and to learn initiative and leadership that was the equal of any group encountered.

A Stroke Group

The Five-Stage group has been used with participants who had sustained strokes. Some characteristics of the members of these groups that have been observed by this therapist appear to be a reluctance to attend groups, the bearing of an emotional distress that was difficult for members to verbalize, the sense of a gravely injured body image, and the diminished ability to physically accomplish what they wished to do. Expressed pain and other limitations accompanied a demeanor that reflected anger, frustration, anxiety, and an awareness of a constantly grim reality. A group composed mostly of members with these characteristics do not coddle a therapist as other populations may. The therapist soon knows whether her suggestions and plans meet the needs and expectations of group members. The Five-Stage group offers a chance to practice movement, accomplish concrete tasks involving perception, and an opportunity to talk about feelings. It also may prevent isolation as members must make the effort to say "hello," acknowledge others, and take leave of others.

Perhaps stemming from diminished ability and the wish to be elsewhere, group members demonstrate a reluctance to move or to enjoy movement. However, it can be very motivating when members are provided with a baton, a cane, or a nerf ball, for example, and they find the involved hand can be integrated into the activity as well. At first, the involved hand may slip off easily; shortly, the ability to hang on bilaterally for longer and longer periods occurs.

Using a routine of exercises instead of functional movement may be more acceptable to participants who do not wish to incorporate the change or novelty movement may represent into aspects of their everyday life. However, they already have been exposed to exercise and now they need practice to move functionally. A compromise may be reached by moving slowly with a few items until they become familiar with it. The therapist can also provide clear explanations of functions the movement may serve, ie, preventing pain and stiffness, and increasing strength and range in little or big joints so that members can reach for objects they need. The therapist can include in the explanations whatever else is noted to be limited in function in group members as she designs the movement.

Many of the members demonstrated difficulty in viewing life as having any fun in it. Holding on to every shred of pride caused them to view some of the activities as being at "kindergarten level." It is with these groups that I try to produce the most adult kind of tasks that are to be presented in the most adult kind of way. Even though I may not be in agreement with such perceptions, I try to second guess how a task might be perceived, using the criteria of "adultness" or "age appropriate." Toby Goldschneider, COTA, a co-therapist, introduced to one such group an activity that proved over and over again to be a success. A large paper bag, holding unusual work tools from her husband's hobby bench was passed from member to member. Getting an item out of a bag required much problem solving for some members in the group. Trying first to guess what the item was by touch alone was requested. When this was not successful, vision was used. If the individual still did not know what it was, another could help out. This activity seemed to reach everyone in the group in a most positive way. Such functional tasks, as putting a plum in a small plastic bag and tying it with a twist tie using one hand, or taking the lid off of a small bean pot to remove some wrapped sugar-free candy and managing to pass it along without dropping it, provided a sense of achievement.

A relatively recent group of stroke patients consisted of two men and three women, between the ages of 65 and 80, who resided in a long-term care facility. The group met once a week for 7 months. My objectives for this group were to attend to the above observed characteristics, ie, obtain overall good posture during group session, improve motor planning as observed by success with tasks, promote appropriate socialization as observed by laughter, expressions of nurturing to each other, and lingering after sessions. To achieve these objectives, activities were selected that would increase the sense of an integrated use of both sides of the body, promote positive equilibrium reactions, and encourage good positioning throughout the group sessions. In this manner, an improved body scheme and body image may be influenced. Providing motivational activities along with the above can contribute to success in mastering the motor planning of graded tasks or demonstrating physical accomplishments that carry over functional attributes. Apportioning time for verbal expression to learn, laugh, and share with others may reduce depression in members and offer needed socialization that they are reluctant to seek.

Although group members had no difficulties expressing themselves when making observations on external matters, no one in the group displayed willingness to own their own feelings or to initiate offering comfort to another. This changed little. It is difficult to affect such a persistent and resistant factor in such short periods. Two members had attended other groups that emphasized such discussions of feelings and had resigned from these groups after a short time. During the cognitive stage, whenever such activity was introduced that required a participant to "say something nice about yourself," "say something about yourself," "make one observation about your neighbor," or allow for any light personal revelation such as, "what makes you happy." The group rebelled with, "We don't want to be psychoanalyzed." Occasionally, some praise or small word of comfort was given to another member and this could be encouraged by therapists with some success. Group members responded with more energy to reading poetry, talking about pictures of nature or local historical sites, jokes and riddles, and reviewing the group's activities for that session. To combat the chronic complaints, an individual member's complaint would receive some intervention from the therapists, but this would not convince group members that sharing and talking about difficulties could bring positive results. This demonstrated how painful and deeply buried their feelings of loss were. Members appeared to use the negative energy of holding onto chronic complaints by adding to them.

Especially for the aphasic patient, a group is necessary for the human contact it provides and the experience it promotes in making oneself understood. Although Eggers is recommended for her excellent ideas for groups of stroke victims, she made her criteria for group membership too narrow. (Eggers, 1987) When a group emphasizes process around activities, the aphasic can be at his most advantageous position because the challenge is to get across meanings in a physical way. There may be some awkwardness during the cognitive stage or more verbal periods but the challenge may provide opportunity. In the group described, it was the aphasic group member who, although she never regained speech or the functional use of her right arm, was discharged to independent living in her own care. She found a way to make her needs known. She chose to come to the group long after she was discharged from physical therapy; however,she would rarely attend the recreational events or initiate socializing with others. Therefore, it may be assumed that a good level of comfort, trust, and safety was present in the group.

Our objectives were achieved to a limited extent. Four of the group members displayed some physical improvement in overall mobility and, during sessions, maintained very good postural stability. No one was less mobile. There was more alertness and more calmness experienced at the end of each session as determined by the therapists. Group members usually lingered at the end of the session and expressed that nothing else was waiting for them, although this was inaccurate as other programs were available in the facility. No visible change in overall attitudes appeared to occur. The group disbanded when one member moved out of state, one was discharged to independent living, another returned to individual physical therapy, and one became too ill to attend. The remaining member expressed interest in joining another similar group.

The Mental Health Group

To promote an enduring recovery from prolonged mental illness, there has to be provision of a consistent and supportive discharge plan attending to the multiple needs of daily living. Not only is this an individual plan, differing from one person to another, but there is a strong demand for a great variety of possible resources in the community so that plans may be individualized. Although this is understood, rarely is there enough staff or community resources that can satisfy creatively all the requirements that exist within the recovering discharged population. Work service programs that offer an array of services from work adjustment to supported employment are one kind of community resource that has many advantages. A variety of jobs are available, usually on a piecework basis, such as packing, sorting, counting, or simple construction kinds of work. These offer the opportunity to practice skills, such as concentration, problem solving, initiative, and to assume a variety of work-related responsibilities. Endurance, such as needed for standing or sitting and work tolerance, can be measured.

One such group of individuals, of which a majority were discharged within the past year from a state psychiatric institution to an intermediate facility, come from that facility to a community work service program for a 5-hour work day. Others in the group live in the community but have a long history of psychiatric interventions. They all meet in a group session for a half hour, three times a week, in the mid-afternoon. The purpose of the group is to promote socialization with a vocational focus. The vocational focus promotes the selection of a variety of related topics to discuss, as well as setting limits for introducing details of personal information that cannot be addressed adequately in the short group session. I have acted as facilitator for this ongoing group for the past 9 months. As few as six persons may attend or as many as 11. There is almost an even number of men and women. Membership changes as people may leave the program voluntarily or are placed in supported employment, temporary, part-time, or full-employment. At least 60% of present membership have attended for the 9 months. Membership is recommended, but no one is reminded to attend. Previous facilitators conducted the group in an informational-educational style that met many needs. Some of the perceived and stated needs of the group to:

- Feel good about themselves, feel greater confidence and self-esteem;
- Build competence in money management;

- Feel hope and interest in the work they are doing;
- Be able to relax and to handle stress on the job;
- Understand good nutrition;
- Develop effective communication skills;
- Find and hold employment in the community.

The first 2 months consisted of describing and demonstrating relaxation methods, bringing in articles of general vocational interest, looking at want ads, and sharing experiences in interviewing or using the daily events in the work setting as a focus for discussion. Movement activity was offered by the therapist. The group emphatically stated that they were not interested in exercise as they were too tired at this time of the day. Nor would they appreciate any no smoking rules during the session. I asked what kind of exercise they would prefer. One answer provided was "weights." From that time on, I filled my cart with weights used in gyms, ranging from 1 to 8 lbs, and two jump ropes. I included a pitcher of mountain water, which I am instructed by members not to forget again when I did lapse once or twice. Sometimes a number of members fell asleep. When this was discussed, the reasons given were that they had worked hard that day, had too much medication, or had had a previous sleepless night. No one admitted any disengagement with the topic or boredom, which seemed possible as well. The weights and the water appeared to help with this sleepiness, which occurs with three individuals in particular.

Group members express themselves but are repetitive, display a limited vocabulary and concrete thought, and appear unable to generate options on their own. They do not listen to each other, nor are they able to paraphrase what it is they do hear or read. Their usual remarks relate only to themselves, with a rare comment on what another has said. Their writing style is very poor as indifference to sentence structure is observed. Yet, most have attended high school and some have had introduction to a community college.

The structure for this group varies so that a Five-Stage approach has been used for a time and, sometimes, it is an unstructured verbal group. However, weights and water are regularly offered to the group members. When a "here and now" issue such as a national election, a traumatic event such as the tragic suicide of a staff person whom some of the group members had known, or an obvious need to vent some feeling about work on a particular day are presented, a verbal group is conducted. The Five-Stages are used only when the session naturally lends itself to this approach and a description of this follows.

The group agreed to use the subject of nutrition as a focus. This continued for about 4 months and the Five-stages became a means of structuring the group during this time. The thrust was to feel good about oneself through greater awareness of nutrition. The written protocol was titled "Be a Healthy Employee" and the workbook used for general purposes was *Nutrition and*

Health (Developmental Learning Materials). When the group sessions began, members were greeted warmly and attendance was taken. The purpose of meeting was stated briefly each time. Also considered as a part of Stage I, the fresh water was independently used or served by a self-elected group member. In Stage II, the therapist used the weights (about 6 lbs on a rod) and they were passed around, or each one was given a weight so all may move together with one group member leading. Some jumped rope. Reinforced frequently were that activity and movement were necessary adjuncts to good nutrition and feeling good about oneself. It was clarified at the appropriate times how exercise was required for any reasonable diet to work, as well as necessary for the increase of calcium and the control of cholesterol in the body. Stage II lasted about 5 minutes. Stage III consisted of using worksheets, related readings, reading out loud, and comparing foods, pictures of foods to classify, and definitions of terms such as cholesterol, vitamins, and proteins, etc. For perhaps two members, it was a necessary review; for others, it was new learning. Stage IV consisted of a more personal kind of discussion as to how individuals relate to information just acquired, sometimes poetry, cartoons, or comic strips were read, or pictures were titled to encourage more reflection on the part of the group. This encouraged humor as well. Hagar, in the comic strips, usually talks about food and these were copied and distributed to the group. Another time, introducing the picture of a little boy sitting in a barn cuddling a new-born lamb and feeding the lamb bottled milk, elicited the title of "Break Time" a familiar, welcomed call to group members in a work setting. Stage V consisted of a formal leave taking in which the group stood, held hands, and a group member volunteered to offer an appropriate prayer or other message for the group.

To evaluate the outcome of the nutrition sessions, a self-reporting questionnaire was used. Judging from the results, my conclusion was that the learning of nutritional facts remained superficial. How to learn and integrate experiences and information for generalization are problems with group members. However, some gains to be considered were that two members credit the group sessions with a greatly needed weight loss. One group member, who needs to lose weight and learn about good nutrition, has withdrawn from a traditional weight loss group conducted in the facility where she lives, but consistently attended this group. Furthermore, considerable time was spent in focused, appropriate sharing, that resulted in a greater degree of apparent cohesiveness which will be described in a discussion on habits. With a flexible structure of a warm welcome, some physical action, focused sessions, simple worksheets, and planned discussions with befitting closure, no one fell asleep or felt threatened in an area where most needed to change poor habits. This procedure follows what is known about the neurophysiological aspect of learning. When the important structures of the central nervous system are stimulated appropriately, an adaptive response is encouraged. (Ross, 1987)

One important goal of such a group is to encourage group members to continue to come together. This provides the greatest likelihood for the possibility of change over a long period. Attendance remained regular for this voluntary group.

Addressing poor habits and the need for change, one special tendency to plague all group members is a stubborn kind of non-relatedness that is the bane of mental illness. This habit is observed in the deeply ingrained self-enteredness of responses, so that no discussion progresses without the intervention of the therapist to paraphrase or call on specific members to react. All remarks are addressed to the therapist. A passivity encumbers group members as participants wait for external direction. Therefore, a great effort was put forth to alter this and to invite group members to learn to use the group and each other as a means to grow. Of course, all types of groups have this purpose. The difference here is that using a variety of sequentially planned activities, as the Five-Stages require, attends to the concrete involvement needed to learn by doing, writing, hearing, seeing, and touching all at once. A small but positive change is developing in the group as members describe their needs, monitor the time they take, and give their reaction to what was said without constant prompting from therapist. When the group had determined, after 4 months, that nutrition had been discussed sufficiently, the members assertively agreed to terminate this topic.

Sometimes, it can be arousing to the group to open a session with, "Does anyone wish to share what your day was like?" This is a good start for the practice of interpersonal interaction and expressive communication. Routinely, however, this does not sufficiently promote enough self-generating inner propulsion to overcome the degree of inertia group members demonstrate. The therapist's constant intervention is required for achieving some nebulous gain in an unchartered course. Starting with such a question can be useful for a group composed of a membership who have known previous stability, and they will develop their own direction. Using the Five-Stages, the therapist also must intervene, but she can come with more preparedness to do this. Specific goals can be developed and the results observed. This level group appears to need more help to organize thought and to prepare for action. Assigning a block of time to a major topic makes it possible to offer it many many times in many different ways. Providing it in a special structured manner can sustain interest, not only psychologically but also to meet physiological needs that contribute to the impetus for learning to take place if change is to occur. Some measurable results have occurred; much more needs to be accomplished. Specific research is required to establish the outcome precisely.

A series of major topics for this group to choose can be taken from their suggestions and structured in a similar way to nutrition. These can be consumer buying, how to find and successfully hold employment, and how to use resources that provide general information, transportation information, or housing information, to name a few. (DLM) All of these have a vocational focus and can provide the needed experience in appropriate and successful socialization.

A Geriatric Group

A geriatric group can be an enriching experience for a therapist because its composition may consist of all the characteristics of previous groups described. Thus, therapists need a greater fund of strategies to meet this greater variety of characteristics. In addition, therapists require knowledge about the "uniqueness of the context of aging," (Hasselkus, Kiernat, 1989) and how to adapt strategies to that uniqueness.

A typical group may be composed of one or two men to four or five women, due to the larger ratio of women to men in most facilities. Physical disabilities may include one or two who may have had a stroke with some sequelae, others may be in wheelchairs while some have independent ambulation, one may have severe deafness, another be blind, arthritic, or have parkinsonism, to name a very few of the possibilities of chronic physical disabilities. One or more may demonstrate marked depression or paranoia, while some may show early memory changes indicating some unusual situation that bears observation. Sensory deprivation is a "given" condition as the familiar self, sights, sounds, smells, possessions, responsibilities, rituals, and programs now are changed quite drastically in the setting of a facility.

Generally, the abilities of the elderly are underestimated in many areas and overestimated in the area of how they should be able to manage drastic changes. Abilities are underestimated in areas such as developing more vigor, assuming more independence for self when allowed the time, and being able to learn, creatively problem solve, and make decisions. Often they are herded together, encouraged to be passive, and exposed to a silence that is infantilizing. When changes are made in a facility or conditions affect their personal lives, the explanations often are meager or even non-existent. Closure on events may not happen. Feeling unloved, unattractive, or unwanted can go unexpressed. A group session can be a positive experience as it offers the opportunity to relate to these conditions. In the group, good feelings, vigorous movement, occasions for creativity and learning as well as expressiveness can be encouraged. The Five-Stage Group programs this into its structure.

Geriatric groups have been covered in this book as examples of the usefulness of understanding how to provide tactile and proprioceptive sensory inputs, as in the chapter on relevant treatment theories. The Five-Stage structure lends itself to a variety of geriatric groups from high to low functioning psychiatric hospitalized populations. The Five-Stages can be applied to groups in day care and to long-term care facilities with every level of care.

A number of patients with Alzheimer's disease compose many such groups and will be described. Usually such groups may consist of three to six individuals. It is always nice to have an active co-therapist, although this should not change membership numbers. Seating arrangements are important as individuals need to feel safe from someone who may get abusive or need to be near someone who will provide frequent physical help or interpretation of what is being said. Consideration is given to observing who in the group should have the freedom from a posie tying them down, a tray to be removed during the session. Eye contact, warm greetings, and good touch (Ross, 1987) is indicated in Stage I. The good touch can come from one another, the therapist, or a quick use of an object that provides a pleasant reward. Again, as soon as therapists feel that as much attention is present as is likely to come forth, Stage II is introduced.

In Stage II an item is chosen from the list in Chapter 2 to be handed out to each participant in the group. These items reinforce the goal directedness of the task rather than the movement. This may help overlearned patterns or associations to reappear. These items also provide a tactile cue in addition to the visual, auditory, and kinesthetic cues presented. Music may be a distraction if provided by a record and may not be needed. However, if one of the therapists understands music therapy, it can become an essential, delightful augmentation, as live music becomes another way to assist participants to focus. Everything that was described in Chapter 2 on movement and the introduction of items with which to move is applicable to this group. The pace is slow. Everyone is helped to start in the least confusing way that can be chosen. Time is taken to wait for each one to succeed. Eventually, when all are together at any one time, a golden moment is shared in the awareness of knowing they are a part of what is going on. The therapist may use this to intensify good feelings by various means. Pointing out the behavior, calling out names and smiling broadly with respect and encouragement elicits more response. Sometimes, with the short attention span present, two or more different items (see Stage II) may need to be passed out to maintain attentiveness. When the Stage appears to be used to its fullest, I ask if all participants feel they have worked hard enough, would like to continue, or go on to another activity. Usually, it is time for Stage III.

It is my experience that this special population has a special affinity for throwing, so I have a variety of ways to take advantage of this (see Stage III). They can spin and find a color on the Twister cloth on which to throw a bean bag, use the large tic-tac-toe game bought in game stores, or make up a game. I have a large flat basket, which I place on the floor. Each group member is provided with three bean bags, and all are usually successful in hitting the basket. It is then replaced with a six-cup muffin tin. The latter is replaced with a small dish. Fewer participants are successful in aiming for the small dish, but those who are enjoy it greatly; some even get up and bend to retrieve their missed throws. This procedure is reversed as the muffin tin is reintroduced, and the activity is completed with the large flat basket so that positive feelings may be felt by group members as the activity ends. My own affinity is for activities or actions listed in Stage III using single-subject puzzles, a board with nails and loopers, a felt board construct, or passing around a scented or weighted object that can be used in a meaningful way. For example, passing around a weighted mirror one day provided some unexpected lengthy involvement from group members who previously verbalized very little. The request was to tell what the participant liked as her favorite facial feature. (As these group members were all women, here, "she" refers to group members, not only to therapist.) I asked Marie if she remembers what Molly said and does she agree. I asked Jennie if she ever realized how hard it would be to choose between her lovely complexion and her wavy hair. Sparking good feelings of vanity also brings an unexpected level of attentiveness. As we went around again, one member revealed her love for cosmetics, another remembered that her mother always complimented her eyes, while a third described how she drove the men wild, and so on. It is hard to raise members of this group to this level of consciousness with any other item. Of course, it is also a chance for the therapist to take her turn as well!

Stage IV may be ushered in with the additional time given to verbalizations, socialization, and interactions that are a result of Stage III's activities. Or a new activity may be introduced, such as questions that may tap into reminiscences, a rhyme to be read, or a picture. One such picture that was passed around consisted of a large profile of a boy's face with a butterfly alighting on his nose. Collecting possible titles resulted in "The Nosy Butterfly." This was suggested by a member who has severe short- and long-term memory losses and usually begins the group by displaying marked agitation. There is no reason to underestimate the production that might follow selected sensory inputs that are presented in a sequential, hierarchial manner!

Stage V is short. Some hand holding, a reminder that we will meet again, and a pause for the therapist to see what is happening to ensure that it is time to close. Within our group session time, group members have been assisted to relate to others, to participate in one or more activities, and to feel calm and alert at the end of the session. The latter may be seen in their posture, facial expression, verbal expressions, and appropriate behaviors. It may not last beyond the time of the session but, judging by responses, quality time has been offered. The group structure has helped us to assemble a variety of coordinated activities that gives meaning to the time we have spent together.

CHAPTER 9

Treatment
Using the Vibrator

The vibrator is used in treatment in physical disability settings. It is applicable to all treatment groups, such as in developmental disabilities, geriatrics, and psychiatric settings, to name a few, and in settings such as work services, day care, long-term care, and hospital care. Some populations, such as those with mental retardation, show a special acceptance of the vibrator. Persons who may reject other kinds of touch or are suffering from sensory deprivation for any reason can demonstrate immediate pleasure when the vibrator is offered. It is not a treatment tool in itself but a tool that facilitates group members' involvement in treatment.

Value of the Vibrator

- It is valuable if it can facilitate acceptance of your approach, touch, or program by a group member. It can be offered daily.
- It helps the patient obtain successful feedback from his body and helps to get his attention, if only momentarily. The sensation is carried by special receptors in the body that respond to pressure-touch and vibration. Some reasons are:
  a. When the back or other areas are vibrated, the reticulospinal and vestibulospinal descending tracts are believed to be facilitory for

extensor motor nuerons. Thus, stimulation may help improve posture.

b. When the vibrator is placed on the chin and moved along the edge of the mandible toward the ear, the vestibular nucleus and associated central nervous system (CNS) nuclei receive enhanced stimulation.

c. In general, gentle pressure and vibration of high frequency, low amplitude go indirectly via interneurons through the dorsal column tracts of the spinal cord to the medulla, and ascend through the CNS as the medial lemniscus pathways. These pathways help mediate cortical control in voluntary movement. These are the epicritic pathways, which invite exploration and esthetic appreciation of the environment. Activating these pathways requires the therapist to follow through with an activity to which the participant can respond by mastering a movement, taking a turn in a group activity, or adding verbally to a discussion.

- As sensory input is enhanced, it may make touch more acceptable. This is basic to the group participant's need for contact with the world around him and helps him to be more interested in that world.
- Group members have remarked that it made them "feel less tired," it made them "feel good." Literature has shown that when used correctly, the vibrator can produce the effect of relaxation which can last from minutes to a few hours.

How to Use the Vibrator

1. Use a vibrator with a low amplitude such as 1 mm and a frequency range (Hz) of 100 or higher. A soft, flexible head is preferable to a hard plastic one. A quiet running sound is preferred to a loud one.

2. Always inform the recipient first that you intend to use it. If he has not observed its use before, a good way to begin is for him to hold it. He can try it on his hand or forearm where he can see and feel it.

3. Indicate that the vibrator will start at the top of the trunk (Thoracic I level). Pressing firmly, move slowly fanning out to the shoulders, and then down the spinal column to the waist. Try moving to either side of column and ask for feedback from participant.

4. Check constantly on how the vibrator is being received by recipient. When the vibrator is used on the back, the participant may be requested to bend forward from the back of the chair, flexing at hip and bringing shoulders forward over knees (this encourages automatic neck extension). If the participant does not respond by bending forward, this can be an indication that the sensation may be unpleasant, he does not understand what the therapist wants to do, or he wishes to have the vibrator just stay around the shoulders. This can be an

opportunity for interaction between therapist and group member, and may even involve other group members.

5. Assess needs. The therapist can judge if this is the time to facilitate needed postural tone in the participant. Start this way:
   The free hand of the therapist is braced on the rhomboids, or just above the buttocks or at the back of the head. The area is chosen that is most appropriate considering the relationship with group member and his size. Therapist can say, "Do you feel my hand?" Pause... "Now, push your body into it." The therapist continues using the vibrator on the back at the same time.

6. It should be made very clear to participant that he is in control and vibrator will be removed if or when he indicates this.

7. Verbalizing how it feels may be encouraged by the therapist asking, "Where do you feel it now—on your right or left side? Do you like it around your shoulders, arms, or on lower back? Shall I move slower?"

8. The vibrator can be used on top of clothes as this is more appropriate in some settings, but if possible the vibrator should be placed on the skin and then turned on. Literature indicates that 10 seconds on and 5 to 10 seconds off may be the most effective way of building sensory receptivity. The therapist should practice this on herself.

9. Two to three minutes of using the vibrator on any person is sufficient. It can be used to unite a group. Some methods are described:
   - Place a chair in the center of the room in which a group session is planned. Invite a group member to sit and accept the vibrator. Other potential group joiners can be invited to take a turn or volunteer for a turn as they remember enjoying the vibrator.
   - If the group has been collected, the therapist can start movement in the group by vibrating one person and asking him, when his turn is over, to change seats with someone else who can come over to be vibrated.
   - To encourage independence, the vibrator can be passed around on a long extension cord to be used by each one as he likes on himself and on others. It is rewarding to see someone who is self-abusive use the vibrator on his arms appropriately, someone else using it on the back of a new friend, while another person tries the vibrator on his own hemiplegic shoulder.
   - When working with younger adults, where the members are more restless and mobile, they may wander around from time to time during the session. The vibrator can be left available. People will use it on their chins, back of neck, soles of their feet, and on the abdominal wall. These are all good receptor sites for vibration.
   - A group of restless and easily distracted young adults who are mentally retarded appear to enjoy joining hands together and

moving in a circle as the therapist vibrates the back of each group member as he approaches her. The slow vestibular movement with the expectation of the vibrator makes the group orderly and calms members down.

10. Any distaste expressed or observed for the vibrator indicates that it should be removed from that participant. By removing it quickly, trust is built. However, each time the therapist introduces the vibrator, invite the unwilling participant to allow its use, as eventually it may be found acceptable and satisfying. The vibrator is a tool to be used in conjunction with whatever else precedes or follows it as it can serve as a reward or an incentive. Using the vibrator is not a program by itself, it must be followed by another activity.

What Kind of Vibrator to Use

The best kinds of vibrators have a Hz (per second frequency of oscillation) range between 100 to 350; and amplitude in the 0.5 to 2.5 mm. Each individual has a different tolerance. For example, amplitudes of 0.5 to 1.5 mm seem to be what can be normally tolerated. However, in a system that is toning down, such as in the elderly, higher amplitude may be required.

I have used the Wahl Vibrator for years with great satisfaction. They have an extensive catalogue and a good customer service policy. As of June 1989, the address is Wahl Clipper Corporation, Consumer Sales, Sterling, Illinois, 800-435-7748, ext. 216. The #4180-003 massager (single speed) produces 20 Hz vibration with an amplitude of about 1.5 mm. The Wahl #4120-003 produces 60 Hz and about 2.5 mm amplitude on the high setting,. On the low setting this massager produces 120 Hz and about 1 mm amplitude.

There are two common types of massager motors. One massager has a vibrating arm inside and the other has a spinning offset weight to produce the vibration. Under heavy massage pressure, the amplitude may be reduced somewhat with vibrator type motors. The Hz may be reduced with the offset weight type motor under load. Wahl produces both types of massager motors—the #4180-003 and #4120-003 have the vibrator type motor. Wahl also produces a Cordless Comfort Massager. Their massager is available in hardware, drug, and department stores. Health-care catalogues also are good sources for vibrators.

Important Precautions to be Remembered

- The vibrator should not be used in the 0 to 50 Hz range as it can cause alarm reactions, nausea, anxiety, etc.
- Drugs alter the effect of vibration. Anti-depressants or muscle relaxants dampen the effect. Participants respond best when they are drug-free.

- The right hemiplegic may find vibration uncomfortable or painful. At the first indication of pain, the vibrator must be removed. Persons diagnosed with parkinsonism, hydrocephalus, and spinal cord involvement do not benefit from the vibrator and should not have it offered to them. Tremor and clonus can increase with use of vibrator in such cases.
- Prolonged use on the skin in one area may cause thermal changes such as redness or slight burning sensations. These kinds of reactions are contraindicated.
- The vibrator is not to be used around or near electrically operated devices, such as a pacemaker, or with a patient on oxygen. When in doubt about using the vibrator in any special disease entity, the therapist should first ascertain its applicability from an appropriate authority.

Vibration is a valuable sensation that, when acceptable to the recipient, never fails to bring pleasure no matter how routinely it is introduced. It is impressive as it fills a void and obtains a response from populations who display sensory deprivation, sensory processing deficits, withdrawal, self-abuse, low muscle tone, and poor posture. To use it successfully requires the same kind of careful observation that any modality requires from a professional.

Information for this chapter was obtained at a vibrator Seminar presented by Dr. Josephine Moore, OTR, FAOTA, and Carol E. Coogler, MS, RPT in July 1980 in Cheboygan, Michigan, from related readings and personal experience.

CHAPTER 10

Reviewing the Five-Stage Group—Quality Assurance and Documentation

Sessions can be reviewed periodically to assess practice and objectives. The following questions will help the therapist to understand what is occurring in the group and what may need changing.

1. List activities presented. What sensorimotor components were emphasized in this session? Was there sufficient opportunity for total body involvement?
2. Did each participant engage (at least minimally) in each of the stages?
3. What was the prevailing mood and posture at the beginning of the group, and how can that mood be compared or contrasted with that at closure?
4. Who in the group needed physical assistance? Was the assistance accepted? Did the assist elicit reactions from other members? What strengths and weaknesses were observed from this intervention or interaction that may suggest other activities?
5. What was the high point in the group? What were the unexpected performances and remarks? Who appeared to be meeting their needs during the session? Which member was least involved? What changes or modifications or activities might this suggest?
6. When did the group appear to be less cohesive or unsettled? If appropriate, was there sufficient time for reflection in the group as to what was happening?

7. When someone expressed a serious concern, or an emotion such as anxiety or anger, was it addressed and relieved, or disregarded in the judgment of the therapist? Recognition of how the therapist responded helps the therapist in self-awareness.

8. When moving to another stage, were group members involved by being asked if they were ready for another activity?

9. Was anyone hurried? Did special kindness prevail? Was praise generously extended?

10. If, during this review, concern is raised about a member's unusual behavior, some unusual occurrence, or the group's disinterest or distractions, is there a plan for a course of action and for involvement of the group in the resolution, if the latter is possible?

11. What changes are appearing in the group, progressive, regressive, or other, over the last 6 months?

12. How do the therapists feel about this session?

The above material is copyrighted and reprinted from Ross, M. (1987). *Therapeutic activity: A neuroscience base for group in long-term care.* In *"The Chronically Mentally Ill: Issues in OT Intervention Proceedings."* Rockville, Maryland: AOTA, pp.48-55.

Documentation

This chart marks the progress of each group member in the Five-stage group.

RATING SCALE

KEY: Behavior seen:
      Almost never—0
      Less than half—1
      Half of the time—2
      USUALLY—3

NAME: _____   GROUP LEADER _____

                      Date   Date   Date   Date   Date

COMES READILY TO GROUP _____

STAYS IN GROUP FOR TOTAL TIME _____

AWAKE/ALERT THROUGHOUT SESSION _____

PARTICIPATION IN 5 STAGES OF GROUP:

   Opening—participant is alert _____

   Movement—performs action _____

   Perception—participates in eye-hand task _____

   Cognition—attentive and contributes _____

   Closure—appears calm and relaxed _____

MAINTAINING SITTING POSTURE OR STANDING BALANCE _____

FOLLOWS 1-OR 2-STEP DIRECTIONS _____

INTERACTS WITH LEADER _____

INTERACTS AND SHARES WITH GROUP _____

INITIATES OBSERVATIONS _____

Goals: _____

_____

CHAPTER 11

An Illustrated Analysis of the Five-Stage Group

Laura McMahon, OTR/L
Linda Sonstroem, OTR/L

The Goodwill Industries' Opportunities for Older Adults (OOA) Program, began operating on August 4, 1986 with a group of eight senior citizens with mental retardation. Currently, the Program is serving 38 individuals and has plans for expansion. The goal of the OOA is to enhance and enrich the quality of life of program participants by encouraging growth in the areas of community awareness and integration. The promotion of socialization skills in group participants advances the achievement of this goal. Opportunities for practicing skills is accomplished through the use of recreation, leisure-time activities, and special groups.

Two Certified Occupational Therapy Assistants were hired on a part-time basis. Their responsibilities included the provision of the Five-Stage Group. The key to the success of this group was its consistent presentation twice a week. Illustrated on the following pages is a group conducted approximately one year after its formation and photographed spontaneously as it occurred. One of the COTA's has since become an OTR.

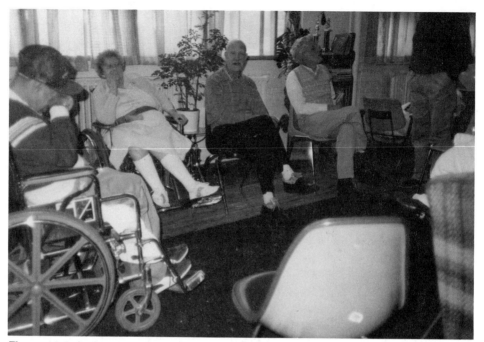

Figure 11-1. At the start of any group, a degree of unrelatedness may be observed.

The overall strategy of the Five-Stage group is to use selected motor, perceptual and cognitive activities in a systematic, sequential way. This organizes members so that they can perform with purposeful, productive, and socially acceptable behaviors. Therefore activities include a lot of handling and passing of items, focusing on central action, reinforcing appropriate involvement with verbal and physical cues, and providing work that is not too easy or too demanding. The pictures and corresponding descriptions of the session demonstrate the activities and the process employed to assist each individual in achieving the program's and the group's objectives. Members remained alert, increasingly became aware of peer needs and, at the end of the session, indicated good feelings through facial expressions, verbalizations, good postures, and appropriate behaviors.

The Five-Stage group method is a planned group approach. Activities are organized and items are gathered and arranged prior to the group so that implementation goes smoothly as the session is conducted.

Seating is usually but not necessarily in a circle. Even at the beginning of an ongoing group such as the one discussed here, a degree of unrelatedness may be observed (see Figure 11-1). Waiting for external events to initiate behaviors can be characteristic. Eventually the group may even incorporate the change of this behavior as one of its goals. Goals evolve as the group skills develop in any area.

Just the action of therapist's sitting down provides a sufficient cue for more focus to take place (see Figure 11-2). This represents prompt association with a very familiar routine that triggers appropriate postural response and facial expression.

Stage I—Orientation

The following goals are to be achieved in this stage:
1. Each member is acknowledged and welcomed in some manner.
2. The purpose of the group is stated or reviewed very briefly.
3. The attention of each member is obtained to the extend that this is possible.

Stage I

When the therapist approached this group, heads came up and turned automatically and expectantly. One participant's behavior affected another as the therapist approached. Not overlooking what is natural to offer gets a lot of good responses.

The orientation continued with a review. The therapist inquired, "Do you

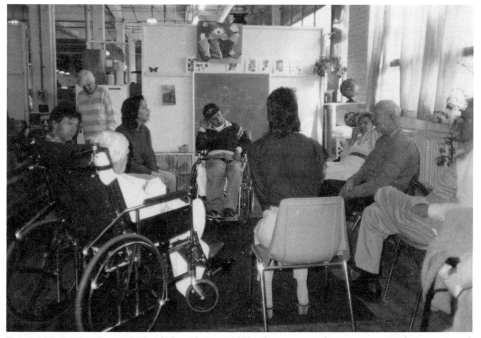

Figure 11-2. The therapist's sitting down to join the group triggers appropriate postural response and facial expression in the participants.

Figure 11-3. While group participants respond physically to the introduction of a marionette, the woman in the foreground, not engaged in activity, sits in a slumped position.

know the name of this group?" Members responded, "The O.T. group" and the therapist continued, "Yes, we meet to help you learn how to do what you need to do in your daily life. If you have something to share or show to each other, you can. We call it your group because it would not be a group without all of you as its members."

To prompt attention, a man marionette was introduced. Group members automatically used head turning, trunk extension, and a steadily fixed gaze. (These behaviors can be contrasted with the woman slumped in the foreground of Figure 11-3 who is not engaged in activity).

Attention continued as the therapist assisted members who worked with the marionette (see Figure 11-4). To encourage a purposefulness she asked, "What is the marionette doing now? Where is he?" This requires relevant action words such as "Lying on the floor." "Lying on my lap." "How?" "Wiggling." This is a chance for new words to be offered and experienced.

No one needs special exercise or range of motion for the neck movement or trunk shifting and rotating that an activity such as using the marionette involves. This is a good physiological progression for the movement that will follow in the next stage.

The ebb and flow of group attentiveness can be observed as each member gets a turn. If more involvement is desirable, members can be asked, "Mary needs more time; do we have it?" or "Are you tired of watching?" The therapist in the group discussed here asked this. She received the answer from the group members, "No, give her a chance." This decision seemed to give the group more vigor and everyone wanted to try using the marionette again. It went around much faster with greater ease, a desirable outcome of learning. Every bit of the here and now is grist for our mill.

Then the group was asked if they wanted to try another activity and Stage II began.

Stage II—Movement Accelerated

Movement activities are offered that, according to needs, alert and excite or calm and relax. These are combined with touch such as a hands-on guidance from the therapist and the distribution of some object to use in movement.

Stage II

A parachute was introduced for this stage. Promoting the shoulder and hand movements initiated in the previous activity, postures were maintained and good bilateral grasps were achieved.

Group members at first called the parachute a flag. This made it necessary to stop and review colors and differences in design.

The therapist asked if it could be folded smaller to fit in the group's circle

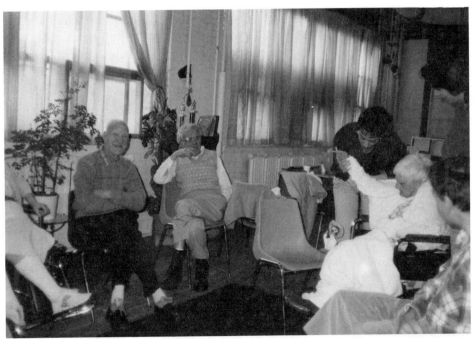

Figure 11-4. Participants respond with continued attentiveness as the therapist assists members in working with the marionette.

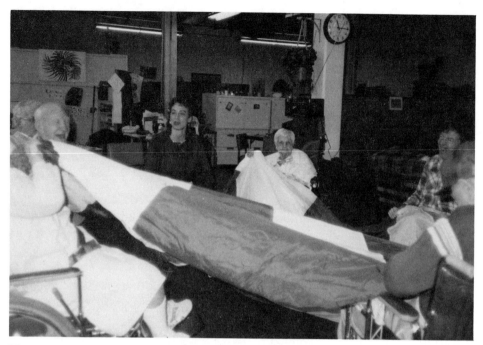

Figure 11-5. The introduction of the parachute into the group promotes good upper extremity ranging as well as increased eye contact.

and checked on who needed help. Good small hand and wrist movements were needed, which required the group members who had been otherwise inactive to automatically get into action. A group member commented that it was good exercise.

Good upper extremity ranging was achieved in using a parachute. Everyone held on, sustaining unity (see Figure 11-5). Those who are deaf get involved in the visual and kinesthetic cues this activity provides. Also, there are many ways to encourage eye contact between members such as asking a specific member to spot another as the chute is quickly raised or raised and placed behind heads.

Smiles are automatic and good movement occurs. Everyone realizes that they are responsible for the chute going up properly or for sponge balls staying in the chute. Objects that make sounds when bounced also can be tried.

Balloons were used with the group being discussed. However, weighted bean bags can be used for greater proprioceptive input and to avoid frequent bouncing out of the chute. Chasing is done most frequently by therapists.

Playfulness and interaction occurred as one member assisted another in a wheelchair to feel what it was like to be under the parachute (see Figure 11-6). This type of interaction is more likely when therapists are less directive.

Good bending, mobility with stability, occurred naturally as a member reached automatically for a ball that had fallen over the edge (see Figure 11-7). He usually avoided such movement.

When it was time to go on to another activity, members assisted in folding the large chute up carefully. Therapists should not overlook the slightest means for member involvement and further learning.

Stage III—Perceptual Motor Activities Offered

In this stage, tasks require less physical exertion and more thoughtful action such as identifying, organizing and interpreting sensory data and making a productive and meaningful response.

Stage III

In using a visual activity, the therapist explained to the group that "There are pictures on the chalk board. Two of each are exactly the same. when you see two that match, put a circle around both." This activity can have other variations. Group members can draw a shape or design and then make an exact duplicate in another place on the board. When each one has had a turn to produce a design, the exercise can be continued as above.

This visual motor perceptual task aroused many spontaneous remarks. The "comb" appeared to be a "rake" to one member and another agreed adding, "Leaves are raked in the fall."

Some comments may become irrelevant. Consider that this might reflect

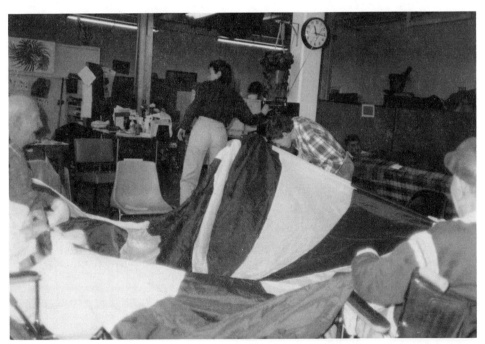

Figure 11-6. The parachute encourages playfulness and interaction among members. Here, one member helps another feel what it is like to be under the parachute.

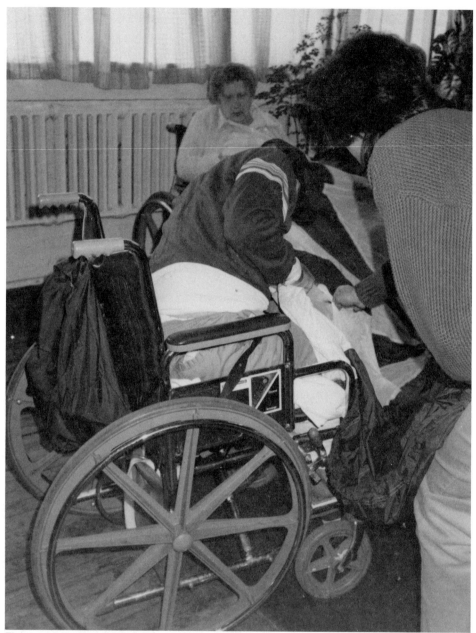

Figure 11-7. A member responds naturally with good bending and mobility with stability to retrieve a ball that falls over the edge.

confusion with the activity, which members do not know how to address. The therapist responded to this by restating the directions for the activity. She reinforced this by pointing and redirecting a member's gaze to where the action was taking place.

Wheelchair clients and ambulatory clients shared in this group. Cohesiveness may break down when the circular formation is disrupted as some members are moved while others have to wait. It can be quickly regrouped.

When a group member needs verbal and physical assistance to accomplish a task such as the chalk board activity, other group members often want to help. Therapists should be alert for creating this opportunity. The therapist in this group called one design a "bucket", others preferred a "jug." The "flower" was seen as a "star" at first (see Figure 11-8). Such little controversies can spark relevant associations and deepen interest. A climate of acceptance is created with the differences. Although the discussion may not seem serious, the message it provides is very important. It reaffirms expressiveness, sharing, uniqueness and risk-taking.

A cognitive perceptual task was introduced to this particular group as a bridge to a brief cognitive discussion. Common objects were placed on the floor.

The therapist introduced items individually and asked for the name of the item. She did this by holding each item up and asking members to identify it.

Figure 11-8. Word association controversies arising from the chalk board activity can deepen interests.

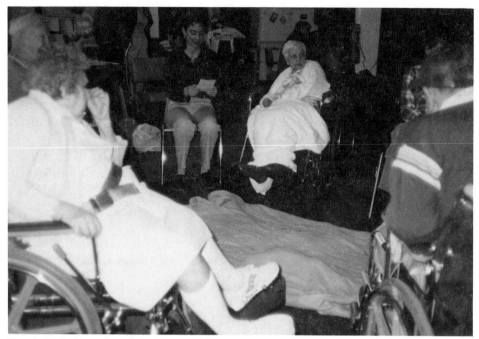

Figure 11-9. Covering the objects with a blanket reminds one member of a grave and introduces the subject of a fellow member's recent death.

When members called the book a magazine, she clarified the difference. Group members were given time to look at objects and to try to remember them. Some members pointed again to each object for a review and the therapist promoted this by affirmation and by waiting before she continued. When the group appeared ready, the therapist explained that the objects would be hidden by being covered.

A blanket was spread over the pile of objects (see Figure 11-9). One member said, "It looks like a grave." There had been a recent death of a group member. In a group conducted earlier that morning, the death had been announced and discussed by the program's total membership.

There are many options to choose from with this kind of comment. Since it had been discussed earlier it could have been left alone. Another reaction may have been to ask, "Does the group want to talk some more about Michael?" or, "Does it remind you of our earlier group meeting?"

Responding to the here and now as observed in facial expression, verbal remarks or behavior becomes easier as therapists gain experience as well as familiarity with a group. Learning not to block out, avoid or deny underlying feelings about any topic does not mean that it is necessary to go into a lot of detail. Therapists must attend in a sensitive way to whatever is required for inner peace and comfort for group members and the group guides us in this when encouraged.

Once the discussion about the death was completed, the guessing game continued. The therapist announced, "If you remember something, go one at a time."

The therapist in the foreground of Figure 11-10 cupped her hand to suggest a cue. Eyes scanned for more cues. They all clapped for themselves spontaneously when all of the items were recalled successfully. They were reminded that they all contributed to make it a success.

At the beginning of the session, desirable behaviors are requested. For example, those who may be disruptive are reminded to leave before they lose control. Others who are known to become restless but can control it are reminded not to wander in and out as this disturbs the group members. Recognizing needs, reminding people of options they have and, with respect, stating clearly what is acceptable can be effective in promoting improvements in group members' behaviors.

Stage IV—Cognitive Stimulation

In this stage, therapist guides members to use the energy created in previous stages to focus on a cognitive task. This is an opportunity for organized behaviors to be observed.

Figure 11-10. The therapist signals the return to the guessing game by clapping her hands. Members applaud spontaneously when they successfully recall all of the items.

Figure 11-11. When asked to discuss their feelings about the group time, members assume thinking poses and display a high interest level.

Stage IV

Memory, fundamental to cognition, was exercised by requesting a review of the sequence of activities presented. The group was encouraged to say what they liked or learned during group time. These requests were more demanding than any required previously. At this time therapists try to focus on each individual in a special way with positive observations.

Everyone assumed a thinking pose, faced in one direction and displayed a good interest level. A therapist pointed to a cue to prod memory (see Figure 11-11). Providing selected stimulation in a systematic way demonstrates sustained interest and desirable behaviors that can continue throughout a 50-minute session.

Stage V—Closure

Brief activities are appropriate at this time so that the benefits of external accomplishment and inner equilibrium may be experienced fully by group members.

Stage V

A great variety of ways to use activity exists by which people may be greeted in groups. This group opened with a handshake and eye contact and closed in the same manner. The opening activity, be it "signing", using a foreign phrase, saying one's name to a musical tone or in a limerick, to cite some examples, may be repeated at the closing of the session as appropriate. At the end of this group, members were relaxed with some involvement. This session had started with little interrelatedness and some solemnity. By the end of the session, participants were more animated and the following remarks were heard, "I do so good!", "I'm ready for lunch", "I want some help." Little groupings formed as some members got up to shake hands. Good feelings need to be shared.

CHAPTER 12

Assessment
The Smaga and Ross Integrated Battery (SARIB) Assessment

Brenda Smaga, MS, OTR/L
Mildred Ross, OTR/L

Introduction

The previous assessment (Ross, Burdick 1981) has been used in part or whole since its inception about 10 years ago. Its usefulness will be described, especially in a retrospective study. The decision to revise the assessment strengthened it. Ten years of clinical experience using the assessment suggests that the test items relate to the foundation skills demanded in daily performance. As the level of ability to participate in daily tasks diminishes, the ability to perform the test items also diminishes. **The reader is advised, very strongly, that so far this assessment is based on clinical experience and a present resource search. The assessment has not been exposed to reliability and validity studies and this is being planned.**

The primary purpose of this assessment is to evaluate clients with low functional ability for placement in similar ability groups. Understanding the collective group profile provides a base level for the selection and presentation of activities so that each member benefits from the group experience. More specifically:

1. **Test results suggest the kinds of activities that can be used with the adult appropriate to his skill level.** Treatment modalities begin at one level and move sequentially to the next. For example, if an individual displays balance problems, treatment activities provided will focus on standing with a broad base, doing some weight-shifting while holding on, before trying activities that require moving backwards, raising one foot, or straddling objects.
2. **In some instances the assessment may display the reason for dysfunction.** For example, disinterest in performing a task may be due to auditory perceptual problems, postural discomfort, distractibility, memory, or visual deficits.
3. **Results can determine if further testing is necessary.** For example, a referral may be necessary for further psychological, neurological, hearing or visual tests.
4. **The test results help the therapist select measurable treatment goals that will be incorporated in the comprehensive treatment plan.** For example, with the problem on balance, the measurable treatment goal may read: When standing with a broad base, the adult demonstrates sustained balance while performing activities selected by the therapist. The next goal to be accomplished might be: While standing with a narrow base and holding on, the adult demonstrates balance while performing weight shifting and postural adjustment activities planned by the therapist.
5. **Analysis of the coping behavior of the individual during testing helps determine what kind of cues and structure will help him succeed.** Observations that the therapist will make while giving the assessment yields information on the degree of persistence, kind of organizational skill and the strengths that each adult uses to meet the challenges provided in the assessment. This information can be transferred to strategies for use when the adult is approached in group. Analysis of the following questions for the therapist, e.g.: Does the adult cooperate only when sitting? Does he like being touched? Does he respond better to aural or visual cues? Is he careless in approach to tasks only when he believes he cannot master those tasks?
6. SARIB can be used as a retest to show change.

Reason for Updating Assessment

Each test item was scrutinized for its value and explicitness. This resulted in developing standard procedures for all test items and clarifying the purpose for each task.

To maximize the time used for testing, tasks were selected that would yield information in multiple areas. The test measures of physical and cognitive functioning skills are dependent on an intact central nervous system. These abilities are the structural blocks for daily living tasks and thus the assessment is comprehensive in scope. Also, as the test was used, there arose the need for additional information in certain areas such as postural security, memory, and motor planning. Therefore, these areas received more attention and assessment tasks were broadened to include these in the battery. Future plans include a statistical study for reliability and validity.

At this point a retrospective study on a single case will illustrate some of the observations that evolved in using the previous assessment.

Retrospective Study of a Single Case

In 1979, Sarah Lovit resided in a long-term care facility on the wing providing service for the highest functional clients. She was independent in such self-care activities as grooming, preparation of an individual dish of food, mending, laundry, and in her mobility. On the 1979 assessment, when she was 93-years-old, she scored four checks as inadequate out of 22 rated skills. This small number of impairments clustered in the area of vision and hearing with some problem emerging with balance. At age 103, in 1989, Sarah scored 16 checks in the impaired catagory out of the 22 rated skills in the former assessment. At this time, her strengths lay in the somatosensory area such as proprioception, finger identification, and stereognosis. The larger number of impaired skills clustered in the areas of cognition with greater losses in vision, hearing, and balance. For example, she showed partial impairment in the Llorens' Test and was unable to perform the Elizur Test, the person drawing, and in comprehending a paragraph read to her. At this time, using her somatosensory strengths, Sarah can undress herself, wash her face and hands, toilet herself, and feed herself neatly when food is cut up and presented one dish at a time. She requires assistance for other functions and even help to initiate. She uses a walker and requires guided assistance to go more than 10 feet. In this way the skills evaluated as impaired appear to correlate with her dysfunction since as function declined, performance in the assessment declined as well.

Sarah is aging within the normal aging process and she does not have any chronic disease. Upon observing Sarah's performance, a large factor of her failure to perform appears to be related to memory processing, which is slowing gradually (especially in storage and retrieval of information) and in which new learning is rare. Sarah appears to have forgotten and needs to be cued for many things she was able to do in the past. For example, she cannot remember how to crack or beat an egg and needs to have her hand taken through the motion. She tries very hard to do what is expected. She partially succeeds but still fails to connect all the motor components of the movement that would achieve the kind of job she used to do. There is no reason to believe that this is due to any form of dementia but is a natural decline.

Since some long-term memory is retained by Sarah, in what context is this type of functional memory useful to her? **Functional memory,** as used here, is relevant and useful memory in which the individual is oriented to his person and understands the occurring environmental event, such as attending a party, having a bath, or being in a car. Awareness exists of the meaning of the event and associations can be tapped. A component of functional memory is functional performance. Functional performance may be considered the ability to start, sustain, and complete the action once the task has been organized and arranged for the individual. For Sarah, functional performance may be considered impaired as she sometimes requires the extra physical or verbal prompt and even more explanation. If provided with batter to stir, she will laugh and say she has forgotten how to do it, but recalls when once started in the motion.

In this example of Sarah Lovit, functional memory is considered as impaired in the context of her current living environment. She lives with her daughter and son-in-law and requires supervision. She cannot learn new information or adjust on her own to changing situations. General events can be recalled but lack details. For example, when asked what had occurred the previous evening, she answers, "We had company, ate, and talked a lot in the living room." Names, particular foods, or topics cannot be recalled. Or she will say, "I had breakfast. It was good and I liked the soup best." "Soup" referred to cereal a word that escaped her. She will substitute the word "cracker" for toast; she always manages to come up with a relevant word. Sarah is well aware that she ate, drank, and feels "full." Despite the failures in memory, her conversation will make sense to the listener.

This retrospective study reinforced the importance of memory and function and its necessity to be evaluated. Research is necessary to establish the relationship between test questions and foundation skills, and then the relationship with foundation skills and functional independence. Further research may substantiate whether practicing these skills in activities can promote or maintain improvement in function. More importantly, the therapist is provided with information to structure the physical, personal and social environment so that the adult can interact in a meaningful way.

Description of Standardized Procedures

A fixed format has been developed for consistent presentation of each task item. This specifies how the task should be administered. It includes directions to the therapist, directions to the adult and scoring. Further information is given on what areas are being tested and why.

Directions to the therapist explains how she is to interact with the adult in giving test directions. The therapist is provided with a worksheet that can be used to quickly score and write on observations while testing. In addition, a narrative summary format is provided that can be used in communicating results to team members, records, to the adult, and his family. This summary is written in a standard computer form model that can be individualized for a narrative written report.

It is intended that the *directions to the adult* can be enlarged and put on separate cards for easier test administration. The intent of the directions is to maximize successful outcomes. Test directions and demonstrations may be repeated.

Scoring has been so devised that each therapist can use her own experience in determining how the total score may be interpreted in her own treatment setting. The therapist can develop her own cut-off points that will indicate global functioning at the adequate level, impaired level, or dysfunctional level for the population she is serving. This will help the therapist to determine the needs of her groups and to match group members for homogeneity.

The terms, adequate level, impaired level, or dysfunctional level used here to relate to individual test items are further explained. The assessment battery contains 24 test items to score; the maximum that can be received is 48. The authors hypothesize that adults with most of their scores totalling 0 (total score of 11 or less) may be considered in the **adequate** level. They will be independent in self-care and can be relied upon to use proper safety precautions. The adults with most of their scores falling within the 1 category (score between 12 and 22) may be considered to be at the **impaired** level. They will require some supervision in self-care and in living arrangements. The adults whose scores fall mainly in the 2 category (score over 22) may be considered at the **dysfunctional** level. They will require moderate to maximum supervision in self-care and in living arrangements. Therefore a secondary purpose of the assessment, but not less important feature of the SARIB, is that the test also was devised to reflect levels of function that relate to the continuum of independent to dependent living, especially in self care skills. Hence it does not examine the wide range of dysfuntion in its scoring but limits its scoring to broad areas of adequate, impaired and dysfunctional levels.

Although the Elizur Test and the Draw A Person Test are not figured into the total score, they provide valuable corroborative data that adds to the overall profile of the adult. It is important to note that the test item, Unilateral Neglect, uses observations from the Draw A Person Test, observations during the whole test, and field of vision subtest for scoring its results.

Note that for the adult who cannot be tested in a particular item because he fails to comprehend or because he is physically unable to do what is required, a 2 is given as a score.

Rationale and observations clarify what areas are being tested and why they have been chosen. In addition, it provides clues and tips to the therapist to help corroborate judgments about the person's level of function, and presentation of activities in the five-stage group.

Implied in the directions is the therapist's need to establish a sincere interest in the person that makes any individual feel comfortable and safe in responding to requests. Each therapist, it is assumed, will do this in her own style when introducing the assessment and the 24 items. Also, optimum results are obtained in an environment where there are fewer distractions in the surroundings, less noise, and warm interest projected by the therapist. The full battery takes approximately one hour to administer.

THE SARIB TEST: ITEMS AND EQUIPMENT

Test Item List

Range of Motion
Posture and Gait
Balance
  A. Ball Catching
  B. Schilder's AEP

General Strength
  A. Shoulder Strength
  B. Hand Grasp

Propriocetion
Visual Performance
  A. Eye Tracking Ability
  B. Field of Vision
  C. Depth Perception

Finger Identification
Sterognosis
Motor Planning and Coordination
  A. Bilateral Rhythms
  B. Thumb to Finger
  C. Tongue to Lip Movements

L-R Fine Motor Control Test
Auditory Figure Ground Perception
Elizur Test of Psycho-organicity
Draw A Person Test
Memory
  A. Short Term
  B. Long Term

Unilateral Neglect
Judgement
Behaviors that Influence Performance
  A. Psychomotor Behavior
  B. Initiation and Motivation
  C. Performance Time

Equipment List

Dynamometer (optional)
Large Mongo Koosh or volleyball or half pound bean bag
Pencil with a bright pin stuck in eraser or a pen light
Manila folder
Coin, key, rubber band, plastic spoon, a paper clip and a pencil
L-R Fine Motor Control test form
2 - #2 pencils
Elizur Test of Psycho-organicity test kit
8 1/2 × 11 sheet of white paper
Two chairs and a small table or bedside stand should be available
The SARIB Adult Profile

Range of Motion

Directions to Therapist

The therapist requests the adult to stand to perform the test. If the adult must sit, this will alter the score only for the item where hands touch toes. Therapist assesses the ability of the adult safely and adequately to carry out movements that she may demonstrate and verbally describes. As a precaution of the carotid sinus syncope (fainting), movement should be performed slowly in items A and D.

    A. Head is turned laterally from midline.
    B. Hands are raised above head.
    C. Hands are clasped behind back.
    D. Hands touch toes with some knee bend.

Directions to Adult Accompanied by a Preliminary Scoring

"I am going to do some movements with you."

    A. "Turn your head slowly to your left shoulder and back to center. Can you go any further? Now turn your head slowly to your right shoulder."
        0 = Fully to both shoulders.
        1 = Half of range on either side.
        2 = Less than half of range on either side.
    B. "Raise both your arms above your head to try to touch the ceiling."
        0 = Fully.
        1 = Barely above head.
        2 = To shoulder level.
    C. "Put your hands behind your back and hold them together."
        0 = Fully.
        1 = Hands unable to reach to clasp.
        2 = Hands at side.
    D. "Bend to touch your toes. You can bend your knees a little."
        0 = Hands touch feet when standing.
        1 = While sitting, can touch feet.
        2 = Touches knee only.

Scoring

The therapist adds all the scores together of the subtests to obtain the total score.

    0 = Obtains a total score of 0 on the subtests.
    1 = Obtains a total score of 1 to 4 on the subtests.
    2 = Obtains a total score of 5 to 8 on the subtests.

Rationale and Observations

With sufficient range of motion, the adult can physically control the environment. This permits him to scan the environment adequately, reach for things away from him and on distant parts of his body, which enables him to independently clean and dress himself.

Posture and Gait

Directions to Therapist

"The action of walking is rhythmic and apparently effortless . . . . Walking is not dependent on a specific position of the head, so that we are able to look around freely while we walk and even wave to someone. Our arms swing alternately forwards or backwards, due to the rotation between pelvis and shoulder girdle and also due to the transference of weight forwards. As one foot comes forward the arm on the opposite side swings forwards. The arm swing is dependent on the speed of the walking and will vary accordingly. We do not consciously move our arms. The strides are of the same length and speed and the feet make the same noise when they make contact with the floor....It is important to notice that the heel strikes the floor first in front and that the big toe behind leaves the floor last and for a short period both are in contact with the ground. We do not lift our leg actively from the hip to take a step; it swings forward as we push off with the supporting foot. We transfer our weight forwards before the heel makes contact with the ground in front. It is as if we are losing our balance and are only saved by the foot reaching the ground in time. The position which the foot assumes on the ground varies slightly from person to person, but it is important to notice that normally the angle from or toward the mid-line is the same for both feet." (Davies, 1985)

Understanding what normal posture and gait are, the therapist observes the adult sitting, standing, and then walking. Circle all the observations listed that apply. For those adults who cannot ambulate, circle those items that apply when observed in the sitting position.

Directions to Adult

"Please stand. Now please walk to the ＿＿＿＿＿ and back again."

Scoring

Circle each item that applies.

1. Leans to one side;
2. Limbs flexed, internally rotated, and close to side (S curve);
3. Head hangs;
4. Rigid and stiff;
5. Kyphosis (humped back);

  6. Slumped, low tone;
  7. Asymmetrical in appearance;
  8. Posterior or anterior pelvis tilt;
  9. Broad based gait;
 10. Eyes are dependent on watching where feet are going;
 11. Shoulder and trunk instability;
 12. Shuffling gait;
 13. Arms held rigidly;
 14. Walks slowly and cautiously, fearful of balance;
 15. Uses a walker or cane or cannot ambulate;
 16. Other_____

> 0 = Adult stands and walks easily and safely, one item is circled.
> 1 = Walking is impaired, between two and four items are circled.
> 2 = Unsafe, five or more items are circled.

Rationale and Observations

Adequate posture and gait promote and motivate interaction with the environment. Posture affects gait and vice versa. When sitting and standing, good positioning and posture, influence oxygen use, effective movement, and safer movement in the environment. Whatever improves positioning, posture or gait and facilitates normal tone will generate a positive effect on total performance. Positioning needs to receive constant attention in the Five-Stage Group. In this test, only standing posture is scored, but the results will correlate with what one sees in sitting posture.

Balance

Ball Catching

Directions to Therapist

The adult is standing opposite the therapist about six feet apart. The adult may sit only if he is unable to stand with security. The ball should have some weight and size to it like a large Mongo Koosh, a volleyball, or a half-pound bean bag. Tennis balls, thin beach balls, and balloons are not as desirable. The therapist and adult maintain relatively stationary positions. The therapist throws the ball or bean bag to the center of the adult first and then randomly to the adult's left and right side, at shoulder height, and below waist so as to observe the adult's ease in reaching and bending. The adult may use one or two hands to catch the ball.

Directions to Adult

"I'm going to throw this ball to you. Reach out to catch it."

Scoring
   0 = Catches the ball at least three out of four times without losing balance; does not need to sit.
   1 = Fails to catch the ball some of the time due to unstable balance or fails to make appropriate movement or need to sit.
   2 = Adult is unaware of the ball coming at them, or is unable to catch the ball and maintain balance.

Rationale and Observation
   See below.

Schilder's Arm Extension Test (AET)

Directions to Therapist
   The therapist stands in front of the adult and asks him to assume a position. That is, "Briefly, the patient stands with his arms extended, feet together, eyes closed." (Silver, Hagin, 1960, p. 129). The arms are "parallel to the floor but not touching each other. Fingers are abducted" (Ayres, 1972, p. 103). The head is facing straight ahead. The therapist stands behind the adult and forewarns him that "The head is passively rotated to one and then to the other side without discomfort . . . " (Silver, Hagin, 1960, p. 129).

Direction to Adult:
   "Put your feet together, hold your arms out in front of you, and spread your fingers. I am going to stand behind you and turn your head from side to side while you are in this position. Relax as much as you can. This is how it feels. Now **close your eyes** and we will do it again."

Scoring:
   0 = Adult maintains balance, trunk and arm slightly deviate in the same direction as head is turned, chin arm rises slightly (Schilder, 1951, p. 93).
   1 = Arms align with head as it is turned, head slightly resistive to movement, arms drop appreciably.
   2 = " . . . wide divergence of arms; convergence till overlap; flexion of occipital arm; drop of chin arm; body rotates at shoulders or hips, or entire body 'whirls' to delicate passive turning of head; extreme rigidity or resistance" (Clements, Peters, 1962, p. 22).

Rationale and Observations:
   These two tests require the ability of the body to respond to changing positions that challenge balance. Activities of daily living require fine adjustments in stable positioning, which permits the limb movements that are

necessary for accomplishing tasks. Lack of balance compromises meeting these daily environmental demands.

There is extensive literature about the long standing use of the Schilder Arm Extension Test (AET) with adults and children with neurological, psychological and learning difficulties. While the exact meaning of the neurophysiological terms of the response to this test is unknown, the literature describes how the AET demonstrates the degree of intergration of the postural mechanisms, such as the Asymmetrical Tonic Neck Reflex and the labyrinthine responses of neck righting. (Silver, Hagin, 1962, p.129). The movements in the test involve the vestibular and proprioceptive systems, and reflect information about them in changes of tone, postural model, and possible negative emotional response. Schilder refers extensively to his use of the AET with patients in regressed psychotic states, especially schizophrenia. Ayers describes a possible negative emotional response (Ayres, 1972; Clements, Peters, 1962; Schilder, 1950, 1951, 1964). Other research with children showed that the elevated extremity is the one with greater muscle tone and is an indication of the dominant cerebral hemisphere (Silver, Hagin, 1962).

General Strength

Shoulder Strength

Directions to Therapist
With the adult sitting, both of the adult's arms are raised to shoulder height. The therapist first pushes down on both arms against the adult's resistance. Then the therapist, placing her hands under the adult's upper arms, attempts to push the adult's arms up, asking for the adult's resistance. Several trials may be necessary.

Directions to Adult
"Put your arms straight out in front of you. I am going to push down on your arms. Do not let me."

"I am going to try to push your arms up. Do not let me."

Scoring
0 = Normal, strong.
1 = Good, functional ability to resist.
2 = Fair or weak ability to resist.

Rationale and Observations
The therapist should note the adult's ability to co-contract, any bilateral differences, and the quality of the muscle tone.

Hand Grasp

Directions to Therapist

Both hands are combined for the final score. That is, the score of the weaker hand prevails and becomes the final score. If a dynamometer is available record the reading instead (Refer to Trombly, Third Edition, pg. 282, for directions and scoring).

Directions to Adult

"Squeeze my hand as hard as you can."

Scoring

0 = Normal, strong for both hands.
1 = Good, functional for both hands.
2 = Fair, weak for both hands.

Rationale and Observations

Note hand deformities such as ulnar deviation, arthritic joints, injuries, contractures or other limitations.

Proprioception

Directions to Therapist

The therapist demonstrates for the adult what he is to expect so the first movement is done with the adult looking while therapist moves him. In the first movement, the therapist moves one arm of the adult's and raises it in forward flexion to shoulder height making sure elbow is level with shoulder. Ask the adult to imitate placing his other arm in the same position with his eyes open. Now the adult closes his eyes. The therapist moves the adult's limbs quickly during testing and provides a light hold on the limb to maintain the test position. The therapist proceeds with other gross and fine motor movements such as:

1. Place limb diagonally across the adults chest so that his hand can clasp opposite shoulder, making sure arm is not resting on chest.
2. Place limb in hyperextension.
3. Put thumb to index finger.
4. Therapist extends the knee of one leg slightly.

Directions to Adult

"Look where I have your arm; copy this by putting your other arm in the same position."

"Now I am going to move one arm or leg in different positions. You copy the movement with your other arm or leg. But this time keep your eyes closed."

Scoring
0 = Able to approximate all movements.
1 = Able to move in the direction desired, but cannot approximate or imitate one out of the four movements or positions.
2 = Cannot approximate or imitate two out of the four movements or positions.

Rationale and Observations
The adult demonstrates that he knows and has the gross sensation of where his body parts are in space without the help of vision or kinesthetic clues (especially if the therapist moves the limb very quickly).

Visual Performance

Eye Tracking Ability

Directions to Therapist
Use a bright pin stuck into the eraser part of a pencil or pen light. Turn the pin or tip of the penlight toward adult and hold it 18 inches from the adult's face. Steadily move the object a span of 20 inches horizontally across from left to right, then move vertically about 14 inches, and lastly about 14 inches diagonally.

Directions to Adult
"Now I am going to look at your eyes and see how they move. Look at the tip of this pencil. I am going to move it. Follow it with your eyes and do not move your head."

Scoring
0 = Demonstrates smooth eye pursuit.
1 = May lose focus on object at midline but quickly regains it.
2 = Irregular or jerky eye movement, cannot follow object.

Rationale and Observations
See summary below.

Field of Vision

Directions to Therapist
Standing behind the adult, the therapist gradually brings the pencil very slowly into the adult's peripheral visual field holding the pencil about 18 inches from the adult's head. Check where the pencil is seen on the periphery of the adult's vision both on right and left sides. Repeat several times on each

side for accuracy of response. The side with the most limited field of vision becomes the final score.

Directions to Adult

"I am going to stand behind you. Look straight ahead and do not move your head. Let me know when you first see the pencil on your left by saying 'Now' or holding up your hand."

"Now let me know when you see it on your other side."

Scoring

  0 = Adult sees pencil when pencil is parallel with cheek.
  1 = Adult sees pencil when pencil is within 45° from the shoulder.
  2 = Adult sees pencil when pencil is beyond 45°.

Depth Perception

Directions to Therapist

Use two alike pencils. Facing the adult, therapist holds pencils at adult's eye level. One pencil is held about 18 inches from adult's face. The second pencil is held 24 inches from adult's face. Allow the second pencil to go slowly forward toward first pencil, aligning its movement so that it can eventually be brought parallel to first pencil. When the two pencils are parallel, they are about one to two inches apart. (Trombly, 1989, page 459). Note that double vision also will prevent depth perception.

Directions to Adult

"Tell me when these two pencils are side by side." Cue adult at different intervals: "Are they together now?"

Scoring

  0 = Adult knows when pencils are aligned in parallel position.
  1 = Adult believes pencils are aligned when they are within an inch.
  2 = Adult perceives alignment when pencils are further apart.

Rationale and Observations

Visual changes are very certain after the age of 40. Trauma, medications, cataracts, or developmental deficits may create additional changes. Persons with neural impairment tend to ignore confusing stimuli, however, like all sensory organs, vision requires stimulation. There are receptor sites in central nervous system visual structures for other sense organs, such as the vestibular system. Stimulating a variety of sense organs will stimulate visual structures as well.

Adapting the above to group needs is the recognition that there will be a variety of visual deficits in each group. Knowing this will contribute to therapist's understanding of how to present activities. For example, when requesting group members to focus on a central point (e.g. target or marionette) the therapist must consider the continuum of abilities and allow enough time for group members to adjust their gaze. Movement of objects in the visual field should be slow and steady. The field should be well lit and as free from distracting stimuli as possible. For instance, if the therapist moved an object in front of herself while wearing a print blouse, figure ground problems are likely to result.

A good field of vision permits adequate body scan. Group activities promote increasing head turning when visual fields are limited and can affect body scan in a positive way. Head turning, whenever it is requested in movement, also should be a slow movement due to the more frequent carotid sinus syncope (fainting) in the neurologically impaired. Group activities can include judging distances, and exploring with touch the totality of an object to compensate for some of the loss of depth perception.

Finger Identification

Direction to Therapist
Ask the adult to place both hands on the table, palms down. Occlude vision by placing an open manila folder over the adult's hands. Using the pad of the index finger, the therapist touches different fingers on adult's hands. At each touch, the adult is required to point to the place where the touch was felt. Remove the folder so that he is able to do so with one hand touching the other. The therapist can touch the same finger in two different places or two different fingers at the same time. Repeat in the same way but with the adult's hands placed down on table, palms up. About five trials on both sides are sufficient.

Directions to Adult
"Place both of your hands on the table, palms down. Keep your fingers spread apart. I will touch your fingers underneath this shield. Show me which ones I touched."

"Now turn your hands over and we will do the same thing again."

Scoring
0 = Identifies every finger touched.
1 = Consistently fails to identify one finger.
2 = Fails to identify two or more fingers.

Rationale and Observations

This provides a global appreciation of the adult's degree of sensation of touch in his hands. This will affect the way he handles and manipulates objects as well as the degree to which he can perform self-care. Poor sensation of touch may influence the inability to isolate the fingers for use.

Stereognosis

Directions to Therapist

The adult places his hands behind his back while seated. The therapist places one different item at a time in the adult's hand alternating between hands. The therapist may assist the adult in the manipulation of items. The therapist should have a duplicate set of test items for aphasic adults to point to, and ask the adult to describe the object if he cannot name it.

The items to be used are: a coin, a key, a rubber band, a plastic spoon, a pencil, and a paper clip.

Directions to the Adult

"Please put your hands behind you. I am going to put an object in either one of your hands. Don't look. Handle it as much as you like and tell me what it is."

"Now tell me what this one is?"

Scoring

    0 = Names all items quickly and correctly.

    1 = On any item delays response or can only describe.

    2 = Cannot name or describe item or its use.

Rationale and Observations

In the group, the adult is going to manipulate many familiar items and with this sensory ability, has a quick perception of those items. With any degree of sensory loss or reliance on vision, motor planning is affected and fine manipulations create frustration for the adult. The therapist should then stimulate tactile receptors with a variety of large, heavy, familiar objects, items that fit amply in the hand, within the group's activities.

Motor Planning and Coordination

Bilateral Rhythms

Directions to Therapist

Sit opposite the adult. Demonstrate one pattern at a time. Each pattern can be demonstrated once again by the therapist. If necessary, a third demonstra-

tion may be used, using hand over hand.The demonstrations are necessary to be sure failure is not due to lack of experience or comprehension. Patterns are started by both hands being held at chest level. Be sure you have the attention of the adult before you begin the patterns. The two patterns are:
1. Tap right knee with right hand and alternately left knee with left hand. Repeat two more times for a smooth sequence of three patterns.
2. Clap both knees simultaneously and the clap hands together. Repeat two more times for a smooth sequence of three patterns.

Directions to Adult

"I am going to move my hands in a pattern.You copy what I do. Wait until I finish before you begin. Watch this. Now you do it."

Scoring

0 = Can imitate two patterns in a smooth coordinated fashion.
1 = Can imitate two patterns but quality affected.
2 = Perseveration interferes with performance or patterns cannot be imitated.

Rationale and Observations

Observe for smoothness and even rhythm of movement as both hands work together. Observe for asymmetry, associated reactions, and the need for the eyes to follow the hand movements.

Thumb to Finger

Directions to Therapist

The thumb opposes the distal pad of each finger in turn starting with the index finger and going to the little finger. Touch the little finger again starting back in sequence to the index finger. Repeat again several times.Each hand is tried separately. Then the identical action is done with both hands performing at the same time.

Directions to Adult

"Watch me. I am touching each of my fingers with my thumb like this without skipping any finger. Go back like this. Now do it several times yourself."
"Now try this with your other hand."
"Now do it with both hands together several times. Keep going."

Scoring

0 = Performs smoothly with speed and coordination on at least one hand; when performing with both hands, slows movement but can still do it simultaneously.

1 = Begins to perform adequately and then becomes disorganized by the repetition of the movement at any point and cannot continue unless he uses vision carefully for each step.

2 = Cannot perform even after therapist demonstrates hand over hand.

Rationale and Observations
See test A.

Tongue to Lip Movements

Directions to Therapist
As therapist explains what is to be done, demonstrate to the patient with your own tongue.

Directions to Adult
"Now we are going to do something with the tongue. Can you stick your tongue out like mine. Now make it go over your upper lip, your lower lip, and then from side to side."

Scoring
0 = No difficulty seen in coordination of tongue movements.

1 = Makes some of the movements but cannot perform all movements.

2 = Cannot perform; can only protrude tongue.

Rationale and Observations
Observe how this test performance correlates with the other two tests for motor planning and coordination.Oral skill mirrors hand skill in the ability to motor plan. This test provides information on fine motor coordination and motor planning, and the results should not be significantly different from the above two tests.

L-R* Fine Motor Control Test

Directions to Therapist
Provide adult with the test reproduced on an 8 1/2 x 11 sheet of paper as indicated in Figure 12-1. Require the adult to identify each shape and if he cannot, identify it for him. The adult then copies the shape across the paper three times before proceeding to the next shape. No time limit is imposed; however, the test rarely takes more that five minutes.

*Llorens LA, Rubin EZ: Developing Ego Functions in Disturbed Children. Wayne State University Press, Detroit, 1967.

Directions to Adult

"I am going to show you some shapes. Tell me, what you would call this?" inquires the therapist when pointing to the circle and then in sequence down the row.

"Now copy these forms as accurately as you can, three times each, in the spaces provided."

Scoring

1. The first score results use L-R scores as follows:

   The geometric form worksheet is given five separate scores, which can total to a possible sum of 15. See Figure 12-1 as the sample scoring sheet to determine individual scores. Note that samples of reproductions that would earn a score of 1 on the fine motor control may be found in Part A; 2 in Part B; and 3 in Part C. An example of a completed score for an adult is found in Figures 12-3.

   Note that the circle and square are scored together for a score of one, two, or three. The diamond is scored separately for a score of 1, 2, or 3. The composite form is scored separately for a score of 1, 2, or 3. The vertical lines are scored together for a score of 1, 2, or 3. The two horizontal lines are each scored together for a score of 1, 2, or 3. The items are scored for control with which the form was reproduced. Two of the three forms produced by the adult (that is, the two best ones) must meet the scoring criteria to be considered for the chosen score. A score of '0' is given if the person is totally unable to perform the task.

2. Interpolate the scores using the scoring below to be consistent with the scoring of the total battery.

   0 = Adequate, obtains a score of 11 to 15 on L-R test.
   1 = Transitional, obtains a score of 6 to 10 on L-R test.
   2 = Inadequate, obtains a score of 5 or less on L-R test.

Rationale and Observations

This test was developed to distinguish between immature through transitional to mature, functional ability. This is determined through theoretical developmental criteria. Experience has shown that this test appears to correlate visual motor skill behaviors with the degree of structured supervision required in the adult's living environment.

When observing the ability to identify shapes, some idea about the adult's conceptual thinking can be revealed. For example, is the composite shape (#4) described as a circle inside a square inside of a triangle? Or is it called a tent or a house, which are considered as more immature thinking (Llorens and Rubin, 1967, pg. 35). Observe the degree of carefulness in approaching the task. Indicate physical and behavioral limitations that may affect fine motor coordination.

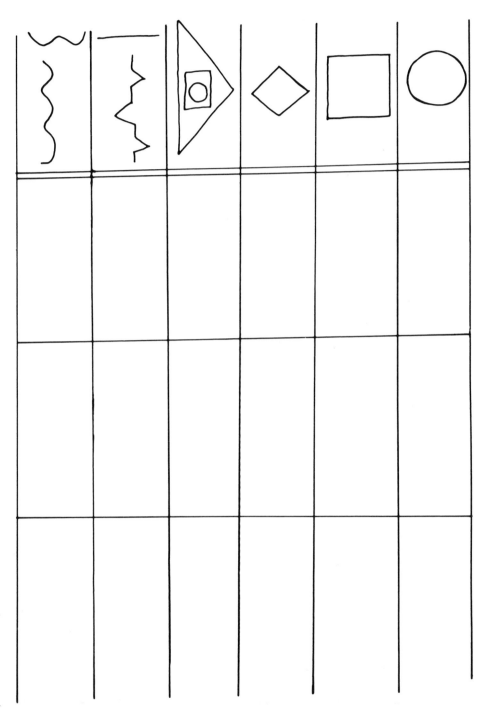

Figure 12-1. L-R Motor Control Test. The square and circle are scored together. Note that the last two figures are sets. The vertical lines, at the left of each set, are scored together. The horizontal lines, to the right of each set, are scored together also. See Figure 12-2 for an alternate testing format.

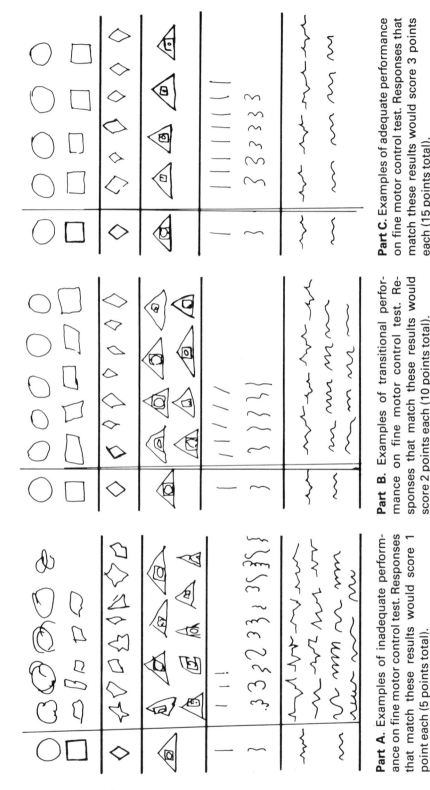

Part C. Examples of adequate performance on fine motor control test. Responses that match these results would score 3 points each (15 points total).

Part B. Examples of transitional performance on fine motor control test. Responses that match these results would score 2 points each (10 points total).

Part A. Examples of inadequate performance on fine motor control test. Responses that match these results would score 1 point each (5 points total).

Figure 12-2. Sample scoring sheets for the L-R Fine Motor Control Test. Completed individual adults' worksheets may contain reproductions from each of the three categories. Llorens, L.A. (1967). An evaluation procedure for chidren 6-10 years of age. *AJOT, 21(2), pp. 64-67, figures 4, 6, 8.*

Figure 12-3. Sample of a completed L-R Fine Motor Control Test. Note that, in the last two figures, the vertical lines are scored together on the left, and the horizontal lines are scored together on the right. Note also that these results incorporate examples of both inadequate and transitional performances.

AUDITORY FIGURE GROUND PERCEPTION

Directions to Therapist

The therapist sits behind adult and says each pair of the following sounds in a normal voice. Do not continue test after 3 errors. Except for the example, lake-like, the therapist should not repeat items if asked. For-Far _____ ; Neat-Neat _____ ; Fun-Fan _____ ; Ten-Tin _____ ; Rug-rug _____ ; Bear-Bear _____ ; Moon-Noon _____ ; Part-Cart _____ ; Sipping-sitting _____ ; Sobbing-Sobbing _____ ; Loading-Loaning _____ ; Tatting-Tapping _____ .

Directions to Adult

"I will say two words. Tell me if the words sound the same or different." The therapist then says "Lake—Like" as a demonstration and asks, "Do they sound the same or different?"

"I am now going to sit behind you. I will say more words. Tell me if they sound the same or different." If asked to repeat them, therapist states, "Sorry, I cannot repeat it."

Scoring

    0 = None or one error.
    1 = Two or Three errors.
    2 = Four or more errors.

Rationale and Observations

The correct sound must be perceived before it can be interpreted, and this exercise can reveal deficiencies that may underlie miscommunication. Note whether the adult turns his head either left or right to hear better, demonstrates or reports a loss in hearing, or reports sensitivity to sound.

Elizur Test of Psycho-Organicity

Directions to Therapist

The Elizur Test is composed of three subtests and is standardized. It takes approximately 10 to 15 minutes to administer. The Manual provides administration and scoring for the test.

The drawing subtest taps the visual motor area. . . . "Performance depends on visual perception, visual memory and graphic abilities." (page 33)

The digits subtest taps the auditory sphere. "Functions required for performance are auditory perception, auditory memory, and voice production as well as prolonged attentiveness. It tests ability to concentrate." (page 33)

The blocks subtest "Provides an excellent tool to tap general intelligence as well as abilities sensitive to brain damage."

Directions to Adult
The Manual provides the exact wording for each subtest. The therapist may introduce these to the adult by saying," Now we are going to do three different exercises. Do you wear glasses?" If the adult's answer is yes then glasses should be worn for the test.

Scoring
"Scoring is objective, easy to accomplish, but requires adherence to directions." Examples are provided after each scoring section to guide your decision. Critical scores are:

Subtest	Cut-off Point
Drawings	10 points
Digits	10/10 or 0/15 points
Blocks	5 points

The Elizur is one of the few tests that is not figured into this battery of composite scores. Its scores should be interpreted separately and should substantiate the findings of the total battery. The three validation studies show that subjects achieving scores higher than the standard cut-off points on two or three subtests can be considered as having problems in cerebral functioning.

Rationale and Observations
The Elizur Test is recommended because it is scored objectively and it is an efficient means to obtain valuable information in the cognitive/perceptual domain. Such cognitive processes as memory, concentration, organization of the reproduction of the designs, initiation, mental rotation of a design, learning approach, and the planned manipulation of materials are required. Some visual motor perceptual abilities are observed as adult views the gestalt of a design, demonstrates spatial orientation, copies a 2-dimensional design to a 3-dimensional figure, and manipulates pencil, blocks, and paper.

The Elizur Test of Psycho-organicity: Children and Adults may be obtained from:

Western Psychological Services
Publishers and Distributors
A Division of Manson Western Corporation
12031 Wilshire Blvd.
Los Angeles, California 90025

Draw A Person Test

Directions to Therapist

The adult is seated at the table and provided with a 8 1/2 x 11 inch sheet of paper and a #2 pencil. Present the paper on the adult's right side and the pencil on the adult's left side and observe how the adult reaches for the materials. It can be clarified that the exercise is not an artistic endeavor but how he views the human figure.

Directions to Adult

"Here's paper and pencil. Draw a whole person on this piece of paper." After the adult is finished the therapist says, "Sign your name and put the date on the paper."

Scoring

This is one of the few tests in the SARIB that is not included into the total score. Its production should be interpreted separately and will add to a greater understanding of the adult. Please note, however, that observations from this test and the drawing are used for scoring the test item of unilateral neglect.

Rationale and Observations

This test provides information about body scheme and body image. The awareness and placement of body parts and the attitude of the adult towards his body is reflected in the production. Persons with disabilities often reveal how the disability exists for them in their drawings more clearly than when they verbalize it. Resources are listed that discuss body scheme and body image in detail.

This is the only activity in the battery that is unstructured. This task requires the adult to organize his thoughts and make a motor response. It demands concentration and forethought which also may elicit feelings prior to action. Thus a hurried performance may indicate poor concentration, lack of effort and subjective feelings.

Memory

Directions to Therapist

This test comprises short-term memory and long-term memory. *Short-term memory* is tested by pointing to four objects in the room and having the adult recall them after five minutes but less than an hour. (Trombly, 1989, page 177) *Long-term memory* related to actual experience and function is tested by asking the adult what occurred the previous evening, trying to elicit sufficient detail for a retelling of the whole event. Cueing is permitted.

Directions to Adult

"Point with me to these four objects in this room. Try to remember them. I am going to ask you what they are later."

"Now we're going to talk about what you did last night." *Note that the following question is postponed until at least five minutes have passed. The next test item can be administered in between.*

"Now, tell me what the four objects were which we pointed to earlier."

Scoring

Please note that this scoring only reflects the short-term and long-term memory tests.

   A. Short-Term Memory

      0 = Can recall four objects after five minutes.

      1 = Can recall two objects after five minutes with cueing.

      2 = Can recall one object with cueing.

   B. Long-Term Memory

      0 = Can retell past event with sufficient detail.

      1 = Can retell past event but without details.

      2 = Is uncertain about the event.

Rationale and Observations

Memory is necessary for learning. It is important to incorporate memory skill building including compensatory methods into group activities. Gauging the degree of memory helps in planning group activities according to the adult's functional memory level. Even when new learning is not possible, associations can be used that build on old learning and are easier to retrieve than new or recent events.

Unilateral Neglect

Directions to Therapist

The therapist's observation of the adult's performance in this battery and the production of the Draw a Person Test are the vehicles used to establish unilateral neglect. Specifically, the therapist can observe whether there is a difference in the adult's response when he is approached from the right or left side. During the administration of this test battery, the therapist should place test materials on the right and left sides of the adult to provide opportunities to observe for possible unilateral neglect. "Unilateral neglect is generally either mild or severe." (Trombly, pg. 167, 1989)

Directions to Adult

No specific directions are necessary as the Draw a Person Test is being used to yield the information needed about unilateral neglect.

Scoring

0 = Adult responds equally to stimuli presented to both sides; in the Draw a Person Test, the drawing includes all of the parts in their proper places and in balanced proportion on right and left sides of the paper. (Pedretti, 1985)

1 = Neglect is not apparent in functional tasks such as self-care, reading, or writing (Trombly, 1989), but the adult may fail to use one hand consistently during this test battery; the Draw a Person Test may show missing parts, may be thinner on one side, skewed to one side, or done entirely on one side of the paper (Pedretti, 1985).

2 = Severe neglect to include all functional tasks.

Rationale and Observations

Unilateral neglect is presently looked upon as an arousal and attention deficit. The therapist pays attention to it because the adult may bump into objects and may ignore events occurring on one side. A group experience promotes moving bilaterally in a normal way because there is naturally a lot of cueing to turn to both sides. Knowing that deficits are there helps the therapist in choosing activities and in making appropriate seating arrangements. Much passing of items can be encouraged that requires the adult to attend to both sides. Bilateral movements that bring both sides of the body into view should be encouraged. Sitting in a small circle where everyone is visible easily helps the adult attend.

Judgment

Directions to Therapist

With the adult seated opposite, the therapist asks a series of questions. The therapist may repeat the question.

Directions to Adult

"I am going to ask you some questions about safety. Think about them. There are different ways that they can be answered. Do your best."

"The food you have just started to eat tastes bad and you are very hungry. What would you do?"

"You have just filled the sink with steamy water to wash in. Now what do you do?"

"You are outside and a stranger asks you to take him to where there is a public telephone. What would you do?"

"The person sitting next to you in the movie theater suddenly slumps over. What would you do?"

Scoring

0 = Proper caution and appropriate action are stated.
1 = Acknowledges risk but action is taken that produces risk.
2 = The response indicates the adult does not understand the risk.

Rationale and Observations

Judgment includes problem solving and decision making that influences how the adult will organize information and take action. Here, actions focus on situations that hold some risk for the safety of the adult or another individual. Grasping the seriousness of the situation, choosing from possible options, generalizing from related experiences, and clearly expressing oneself through language are the cognitive abilities that are required here. Judgment is a crucial issue that often is used to decide dependent or independent living status.

Behaviors That Influence Performance

Directions to Therapist

The therapist's observation of the adult in this battery is used to rate behaviors that influence performance.

Directions to Adult

No directions are necessary as the behaviors observed during the administration of the test items are used to score the three subtests.

Scoring

A. Psychomotor Behavior

0 = Appropriately spontaneous.

1 = Hyperactivity or hypoactivity impedes quality task performance.

2 = Cannot perform tasks due to the degree of hyperactivity or hypoactivity.

B. Initiation and Motivation

0 = Participates willingly in task; self-starting; seeks help appropriately.

1 = Reluctant to participate in task; needs extra cueing to initiate each task; does not ask for help it is needed.

2 = Resistant to participation; shows no interest in tasks.

C. Performance Time

0 = Performs tasks in expected time.

1 = Needs 50% more time than expected to perform tasks.

2 = Needs more than 50% more time than expected to perform tasks.

Rationale and Observations

The above items have been selected because they directly relate to test performance. They do not represent all the behaviors that can be noted on the summary to complete a comprehensive profile of the adult. Social conduct, beliefs and values, general conversation, means of expressing oneself, and insight into one's strengths and weaknesses additionally are part of understanding the total person.

THE SMAGA AND ROSS INTEGRATED BATTERY WORKSHEET
(SARIB)

NAME OF THERAPIST: _____   DATE OF ASSESSMENT: _____

NAME: _____   DATE OF BIRTH: _____

AGE: _____   SEX: M   F   HANDEDNESS: R   L   DATE OF REFERRAL: _____

REASON FOR REFERRAL: _____

DIAGNOSIS: _____ TOTAL **SARIB** SCORE:

NUMBER OF **ELIZUR** SUBTESTS ABOVE CUT OFF POINT:

BODY SCHEME & IMAGE OF **DRAW A PERSON** REFLECTS SARIB: **YES** **NO**

Instructions: Circle, then write the appropriate scoring response in the right side block. Test items are weighted equally when compiling the total score. A score of "0" indicates adequate function in performance of that test item; a score of "1" indicates imparied function; and a score of "2" indicates that the adult is at a dysfunctional level. Note that the Elizur Test and the Draw A Person Test are not included in the total score. Use available space on this worksheet for notes. The adult's failure to perform due to incomprehension or physical inability obtains a score of "2" for that item.

TEST ITEM	ADEQUATE FUNCTION 0	IMPAIRED FUNCTION 1	DYSFUNCTION 2	SCORE
RANGE OF MOTION				
COMPOSITE SCORE	Obtains a 0	Obtains 1 to 4	Obtains 5 to 8	
a. HEAD TURNED	Fully to both shoulders	1/2 of range on either side	Less than 1/2 range on either side	
b. ARMS ABOVE HEAD	Fully	Barely above head	To shoulder level	
c. HANDS BEHIND BACK	Fully	Unable to reach to clasp hands	Hands at side	
d. HANDS TOUCH FEET	While standing can touch feet	While sitting can touch feet	Touches knee only	

© SLACK Incorporated

ITEM	0	1	2	SCORE
POSTURE AND GAIT				
circle: (sitting) (standing)	Stands & walks easily; 1 circle	2 to 4 circles	Unsafe; 5 or more circles	◯

1. -leans to one side
2. **-head hangs**
3. -rigid and stiff
4. **-slumped, low tone**
5. -asymmetric in appearance
6. **-arms held rigidly**
7. -limbs flexed, internally rotated and close to side; S curve
8. **-kyphosis**
9. -posterior/anterior pelvic tilt
10. -shoulder and trunk instability
11. **-eyes are dependent on watching where feet are going**
12. -broad based gait
13. **-shuffling gait**
14. -walks slowly and cautiously, appears fearful of balance
15. **-uses walker, cane, or cannot ambulate**
16. -other:_____

BALANCE				
A. BALL CATCHING	While standing, catches 3 of 4 times and maintains balance	Does not catch some of the time because of balance and movement; needs to sit	Unable to catch and maintain balance; Unaware of ball	◯
B. SCHILDER'S ARM EXTENSION TEST	Maintains balance, trunk & arm slightly deviate in same direction, chin arm rises slightly	Arms align with head when head moved, head slightly resistive, arm drops appreciably	Wide divergence of arms, or overlap, flexion of occipital arm, chin arm drops, feet move as body rotates	◯

GENERAL STRENGTH				
A. SHOULDER STRENGTH Note: R ⊙⊜⊙ L	Normal, strong for both sides	Good, functional ability to resist on both sides	Fair, weak ability to resist on both sides	◯
B. HAND GRASP Note: R ⊙⊜⊙ L	Normal, strong for both hands	Good, functional for both hands	Fair, weak for both hands	◯

PROPRIOCEPTION				
	Approximates all movements	Moves in direction but cannot approximate 1 of 4 movements or positions	Cannot imitate or approximate 2 of 4 movements or positions	◯

© SLACK Incorporated

ITEM	0	1	2	SCORE
VISUAL PERFORMANCE				
A. EYE TRACKING ABILITY	Smooth eye pursuit crossing midline	Loses focus at midline, but quickly regains it	Jerky eye movement, cannot follow object	
B. FIELD OF VISION	Sees pencil when parallel with cheek for both sides	Sees pencil when 45 degrees from shoulder for both sides	Sees pencil when beyond 45 degrees for one or both sides	
C. DEPTH PERCEPTION	Knows when aligned in parallel position	Believes aligned within 1 inch	Perceives alignment when more than 1" apart	
FINGER IDENTIFICATION				
	Identifies every finger touched	Consistently fails to identify 1 finger	Fails to identify 2 or more fingers	
STEREOGNOSIS				
Note: Differentiate from anomia	Names quickly and correctly	Delays response, incorrect response or only can describe	Cannot name or describe or tell its use	
MOTOR PLANNING AND COORDINATION				
A. BILATERAL RHYTHMS	Can imitate three patterns in smooth coordinated fashion	Can imitate two patterns but quality and crossing midline affected	Perseveration interferes with performance or cannot imitate	
B. THUMB TO FINGER	Performs smoothly with at least one hand	Begins, cannot continue; reliance on vision slows performance	Cannot perform even after hand over hand demo	
C. TONGUE TO LIP MOVEMENTS	No difficulty seen in coordination of tongue movements	Makes some of the movements but cannot perform all	Cannot perform; can only protrude tongue	
L-R FINE MOTOR CONTROL TEST				
	Adequate, obtains a score between 11 and 15	Transitional, obtains a score between 10 and 6	Inadequate, obtains a score of 5 or less	
AUDITORY FIGURE GROUND PERCEPTION				
	One error	Two or three errors	Four or more errors	

ITEM	0	1	2	SCORE
ELIZUR TEST OF PSYCHO-ORGANICITY				

Note: Not part of the total score of the battery.	Scores of Drawings:
	    Digits:
	    Blocks:			

DRAW A PERSON TEST				
Note: Not part of the total score of the battery.	Comment on body scheme or percept and body image.			
MEMORY				
A. SHORT TERM	Recalls 4 items after 5 minutes	Recalls 2 items after 5 minutes	Recalls 1 item with cueing	
B. LONG TERM	Recalls detail for event	Lacks detail about event	Is uncertain about event	
UNILATERAL NEGLECT				
	Responds equally to stimuli; drawing is balanced	Fails to use one side consistently in tasks; drawing may be skewed; neglect seen in field of vision test	Severe neglect; performance of tasks affected	
JUDGEMENT				
	Proper caution observed in the action stated	Acknowledges risk, but action taken produces risk	Does not understand the risk	
ATTENDING BEHAVIOR THAT INFLUENCES PERFORMANCE				
A. PSYCHO-MOTOR BEHAVIOR	Appropriately spontaneous	Hyperactivity or or hypoactivity impedes quality task performance	Cannot perform tasks due to degree of hypo- or hyper-activity	
B. INITIATION AND MOTIVATION	Participates willingly; self-starting; seeks help if needed	Reluctant to participate; needs cueing to initiate; does not seek help; very passive	Resistant to participate; shows no interest in task	
C. PERFORMANCE TIME	Performs task in expected time	Needs 50% more time than expected	Needs morethan 50% of time expected	

TOTAL SARIB SCORE:

THE SMAGA AND ROSS INTEGRATED BATTERY ADULT PROFILE
(SARIB)

NAME OF THERAPIST: _____   DATE OF ASSESSMENT: _____

NAME: _____   DATE OF BIRTH: _____

AGE: _____ SEX: M F HANDEDNESS: R L   DATE OF REFERRAL: _____

REASON FOR REFERRAL: _____

DIAGNOSIS: _____

		BALANCE		STRENG				VISUAL					MOTOR						MEM					BEHVR		
		B				P					S				L	A			N	J	P	M	T			
R	G	A	A			R	F				T	B	T	T	-	U	S	L	E	U	S	O	I			
O	A	L	E	S	H	O	E	F	D	F	E	R	T	T	R	D	T	T	G	D	Y	T	M			
M	I	L	T	S	G	P	O	O	P	I	R		F	L	D		T						E			
	T							V																		
equate																										
paired																										
sfunction																										

CLUSTERS CAN BE SENSORIMOTOR, SENSORY, SOMATOSENSORY, PERCEPTUAL, COGNITIVE, AND BEHAVIORAL.

TOTAL **SARIB** SCORE:

NUMBER OF **ELIZUR** SUBTESTS BELOW CUT OFF POINT:

BODY SCHEME & IMAGE OF **DRAW A PERSON** REFLECTS SARIB: YES   NO

Range of Scores:

0 - 11 Considered an adequate level or possessing the minimum competencies for independence in self care and use of proper safety precautions.

12 - 22 Considered an impaired level requiring supervision in self care and in living arrangements.

23 - 43 Considered at dysfunctional level requiring moderate to maximum supervision in self care and in living arrangements.

NARATIVE SUMMARY
The strengths for **adequate** function cluster or scatter in the areas of

The areas of **impaired** function cluster or scatter in

The problems that reflect a **dysfunctional** status cluster or scatter in

Body scheme and body image on the **Draw A Person test** suggest

Other **behaviors** noted that will impact on the treatment are

Additional rehabilitation **testing recommended**

The recommended **long term goal** for rehabilitation is

The measurable **short term objectives** for the next____(days/ weeks/ months)

Short term objectives are implemented via these **groups and individual sessions** with the dates and times listed

Referrals for other services recommended are

Aftercare projected following discharge may include

Signature of Therapist_____Date_____

Levels of Development

The First Year

Newborn to Six months
Simple, brightly colored rattles
Soft balls
Soft stuffed animals and dolls
Brightly colored dangling objects
Mobiles
Objects to look at—pictures, people
Things to listen to—singing, little bells, music, being talked to, read to
Place to be on the floor part of every day
Place to sit up with interesting things to see part of every day

4 to 10 months
More complicated rattles
Nesting containers of aluminum or plastic—cans and ice cream cartons
Spoons
Measuring spoons
Hard rubber rings
Bells to shake
Busy box with knobs, cranks, wheels, and dials for crib or play pen
Cradle gym
Two or three small wooden, plastic, rubber, or sponge blocks
A water toy, floating duck, water ball, or shallow plastic container
Empty spools for stacking
Time each day for listening to stories or nursery rhymes

9 months to 1 year
Large rubber balls
Water toys
A container and things to put in it—oatmeal box with clothespins
Plastic balloons that do not break easily
Picture pages made with cut-out ads pasted on plain paper

The Second Year

12 to 18 months
Push toys for learning to walk
Pull toys once walking has begun
Simple take apart toys
Empty spools for stringing
Toy telephone
Rubber dolls
Soft animals
Balls and balloons
Cloth blocks
Trips to the playground for sand play and swings

18 Months to 2 years
Pots, pans and covers
Blocks
Hammer and peg toys
Rocking horse
Old magazines to look through
A time to listen to short fables and rhymes

Two to Three Years

Continue all or any activities from last group that child enjoys and wants to
    do with you.
Spools to string
Big cardboard beads to string (sections of tissue paper or paper towel rolls)
Scissors and paper
Old greeting cards
Fingerpainting
Shopping, and identifying objects, sounds
Trips to the playground for slides, swings, sand, etc.
Tea set
Broom
An egg beater
Trucks and cars
Dolls and stuffed animals
Rocking and riding toys
Big boxes for climbing into
A pail and shovel (a container and spoon)
A scoop
Muffin and pie tins

Cookie cutters
A strainer
Music
Beads or macaroni for stringing
Picture books

Three to Four Years

Toys that make noise
Paper, pencils, and crayons
Fingerpainting
Playdoh
Dolls, stuffed animals
Doll equipment
Blocks
Old hats, high heels, dresses, and suit coats for dramatic play
Puzzles, crayons, chalk, blackboard, paste
Tricycle
Storybooks
Trips to playground for see saw, slides, swings, climber
Organized play at least 15 minutes sometime during the day
Simon Says
Looby Loo
Trips to the zoo
Bus rides (helpful for the child to supplement experiences in the home)

Four to Five Years

Time to play alone or with two other children
Parties with paper hats, balloons, something to eat and drink (cookies or graham crackers and Koolaid)
Time to listen to stories, poems
Drawing
Pictures to sew
Paper airplanes, windmills
Fingerpainting
Dolls
Doctor and nurse kits
Wheeled toys—trucks and cars
Equipment—empty cans, boxes, and play money that can be used to play "store"
Paper, paste, crayons, paint, clay
Junk box for quiet play

Simple lotto games
Trips to the playground
Trips to the zoo
Time for the child to tell about the day's experiences
Looby Loo
Simon Says

Five to Six Years

Dolls and doll equipment
Jumprope
Jacks
Kites
Small purses
Scrap books
Fingerpainting
Cars and trucks
Woodworking tools
Tricycle
Roller and ice skates

Six to Seven Years

Wagons, trucks, trains, planes, boats
Construction toys
Gardening equipment
Tinker toys
Lego sets
Erector sets
Marbles
Soft ball and bat
Dolls and paper dolls
Sets for sewing, stringing, weaving, and puppet making
Board games
Old watches and clocks to take apart
Story books
Trips to the library

Seven to Eight Years

Tops and marbles
Playing house and dressing up equipment
Jumprope

Bicycle
Skates, skis
Balls
Magic tricks
Board games
Jigsaw puzzles
Paint, clay, paste, paper, scissors
Possibly science materials, chemistry sets, navigation sets, telegraphy, or
   astronomy sets

Eight Years and Beyond

Board games
Puzzles
Materials for handicrafts, metalwork, puppetry, leatherwork, beadwork,
   weaving
Skates
Kites
Active sports equipment
Time for nature walks at parks or the beach
Assorted junk and box to keep it in
Paper dolls
Marbles and tops
Model to build
Construction sets
Science kits

NOTE: Italics indicate items that can be made or found at home.

Assessment

ALLEN Lower Cognitive Level Test (LCL)

The LCL asks the patient to imitate a motor action. The motor action selected is clapping hands because it is familiar and cross-cultural, and the ability seems to be retained by most of the disabled population. Clapping is an action learned by small children that is not confounded by a need to cross the midline. Clapping also lends itself to interrater reliability. Scoring criteria appear in Table B-1.

Verbal Directions

"I'd like to see how well you can follow directions. Please clap your hands loudly three times. Watch me."

Demonstration

At the midline, the therapist claps three evenly spaced beats that are distinguishable and clearly audible. The directions may be repeated one time. The therapist may say, "I did not hear you," when there is some doubt about the claps being audible. The therapist may also help to initiate the action by placing the palmar surface of the hands together.

Setting

The test should be given in a setting where the patient and the therapist can hear the clapping.

The interrater reliability was examined by Heying with four staff therapists at Los Angeles County-University of Souther California Medical Center. Interrater reliability was 100 percent for 22 subjects selected because it was thought they might be functioning at levels 1, 2, and 3. The validity of the test needs further investigation. With the ACL as the independent variable, the LCL gave a false positive (i.e., a score of level 3) to 70 percent of the subjects who scored at level 2 on the ACL. It may not be possible to differentiate between levels 2 and 3 with the LCL; for the present we have discarded the level 3 score on the LCL.

Table B-1
Lower Cognitive Level Test: Scoring Criteria

Behavior	Score
Three audible, consecutive, evenly spaced claps; contact at the palmar surface (May be more than three)	Level 3
One or two claps, claps not audible	Level 2
Other movements between claps	
Clapping initiated between claps	
Attempts to clap, but contact with other than palmar surface (e.g., fist into palm, pads of digits)	
No response	Level 1
Refusal	No Score

APPENDIX C

Alerting and Calming

Alerting and Calming
Through Sensory Stimulation

Senses	Methods Used to Stimulate	Behaviors
Touch		
Protopathic	Rubbing/different textures, self touch	Alerting
Epicritic	Self touch	Calming
Vestibular	Rotation	
	—Fast	Alerting
	—Slow	Calming
Proprioception	Pressure—Light	Alerting
	—Moderate	Calming
Vision	Bright colors—Light	Alerting
	Pastels—Low Intensity	Calming
Hearing	Contrast Sounds—Loud	Alerting
	Repetitive changes—Slow	Calming
	Melodious and soft sounds	Calming
Smell	Pungent Smells	Alerting
	Potpourri of sweet smells	Calming
Taste	Strong Flavors—Crunchy	Alerting
	Smooth texture—tepid	Calming
	temperatures	

Alerting and Calming
Through Music and Movement

Alerting	Calming
Increased muscle activity with increased muscle tension.	Decreased motor activity, relaxed muscle fibers.
Head up, chest out, general extension pattern.	Head down, torso bent (forward flexion), deep breathing.
Light touch, patting, whisking, brushing movements.	Heavy pressure touch, massage.
Percussive movements.	Swinging or sustained movements.
Non-repetitive or uneven rhythmic patterns. Uneven loco motor movements (skip, gallop, slide).	Slow, repetitive movements, axial or locomotor.
Fast, loud music of variable intensity, sharp sounds.	Slow, dreamy, lyrical music; Adagio.
Linear acceleration and deceleration in locomotor patterns.	Linear movement consistency.
Defy gravity, up and down.	Give in to gravity, body hanging, collapse or ragdoll movements.
Fast spinning or twirling.	Slow turning.

Dona Burdick

Tools

Cut-Up Figure

On poster board approximately 24 x 36 inches draw a figure as illustrated below. Draw the figure a second time on another piece of poster board and cut up into large sections, e.g. arms, legs, head, torso, and attach a piece of velcro to the back of the piece so that it will match to a corresponding piece of velcro on the whole uncut figure. Body parts, directionality, and figure ground activities can be reviewed. This has been used with blind patients, stroke patients, autistic children, and regressed mentally ill patients.

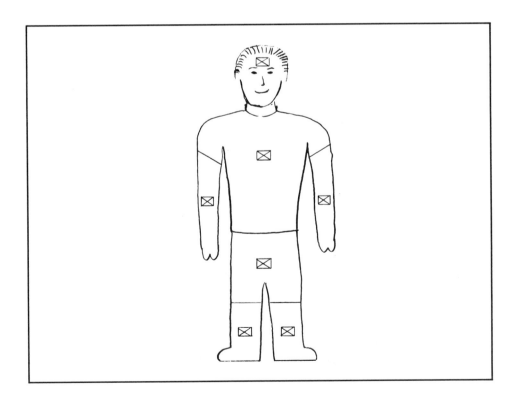

Geometric Shapes

This is another opportunity to work standing and using the floor as a table, which utilizes frequent bending and scanning. These shapes are drawn on a large piece of poster board. Matching pieces can be passed around to patients in a group. The top shapes can be placed down only after the larger one is put in place first. Design it as you will to make it easier or more difficult. Use color if desired. Have players name the shape and color.

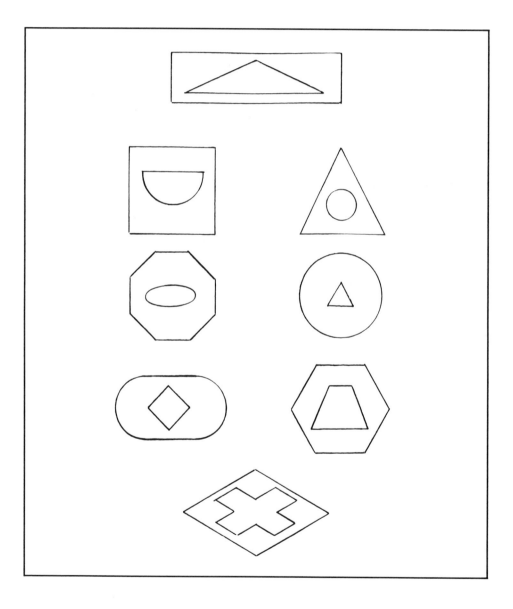

Puzzles

Here is a suggested visual figure ground exercise to be done by a group. Two such puzzles, exactly alike should be drawn on large poster board, since it is to be put on the floor. The second puzzle is to be cut into the sections outlined to be handed to each member to place on top of the matched section. Patients should be standing, so they will need to bend and stoop, wait their turn, use motor planning movements, and cooperate in a group venture.

Holiday themes, e.g., Halloween symbols and color, can be introduced. The group can design them for grade school children as well and send to a particular class. Teachers with learning disability groups welcome such gifts.

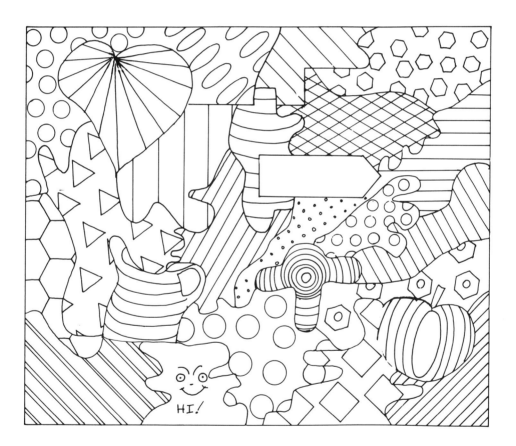

Pegboard

This may be a large or small peg board to use on table, tray, or ground.

Directions

Have patients put pegs in holes according to the sample cards, which progress in difficulty. The therapist should offer three pegs to each patient, and move from patient to patient to develop the pattern.

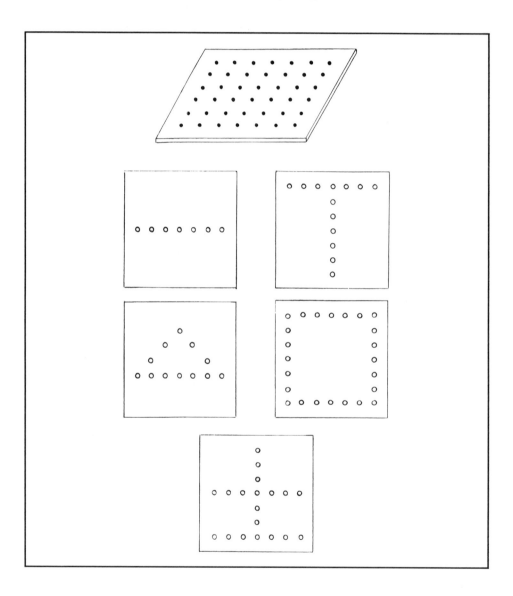

Tongue Depressor Shapes

Activity

Prepare cutouts from colored construction paper of as many geometric shapes as desired. Duplicated each shape in many different colors of paper. The size of the shape is approximately 6 x 6 inches. Paste a tongue depressor stick on each one for ease of holding.

Two different shapes or colors may be chosen by group members. Members may take turns as leaders, calling out either a color or shape for participants to match. Participant may wave what he has or walk into the center of the group with others who have either the shape or color called. Group has to be very attentive to work with these shapes.

A set of these shapes may be made by the group as a gift for school children. The set may include the instructions for use. See sample shape below.

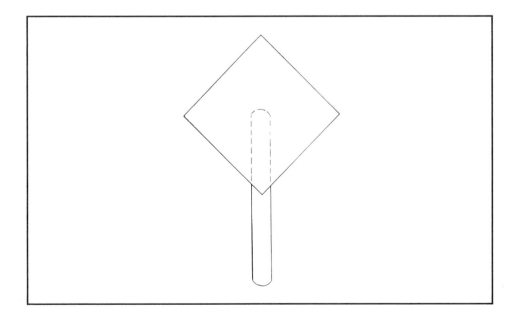

Bibliography and Resources

PREFACE

Fine, S. Letter to author, July 1989.

OVERVIEW

Corcoran, MA and Barrett, D: Using secondary integration principles with regressed elderly patients. This article appears jointly in Sensory Integrative Approaches in Occupational Therapy (New York, NY: The Haworth Press, 1987) and *Occupational Therapy in Health Care, 4(2),* (Summer 1987).

Ross, M (1987). Group process: Using therapeutic activities in chronic care. Thorofare, NJ: Slack Incorporated.

STAGE I

Flaghouse (See Resources)

World Wide Games (See Resources)

STAGE II

Kimbo (See Resources)

Ross, M (1987). Group Process: Using therapeutic activities in chronic care. Thorofare, NJ: Slack Incorporated.

S & S Arts and Crafts (See Resources)

Siegel, BS (1986). Love, medicine and miracles. New York, NY: Harper & Row.

STAGE III

Abreu, BC and Toglia, JP (1987). Cognitive rehabilitation: A model for occupational therapy. *Am J Occup Ther* 41(7):439-448.

DLM Teaching Resources (See Resources)

Computer articles:

Chan, RSK (1988). Attentional deficits in the post-CVA patient. *Advance 4(6)* (Feb. 8).

American Journal of Occupational Therapy; Special Issue on Technology. Vol 41, No 11, November 1987.

Dubuque, TJ (1987). Computer applications startup system for use within a mental health setting. *Forum II* (25) (June 24).

Huebner, R (1987). Computer use in public schools. *Atlantic Edition II* (34) (August 26).

Occupational Therapy News; Occupational Therapy and Computers. (Reprinted from the Administration and Management SIS Newsletter, Vol 3, No 1, March 1987) March 1988, pp. 12-14.

McLean, VP (1988). Using robots in a group with the neuropsychologically impaired: Achieving a sense of control over the environment. OT in Mental Health. *Journal of Psychosocial Practice & Research.* 8(3). New York, NY: The Haworth Press, Inc.

Sunburst (See Resources)

Talicor Inc. (Formerly the Ungame Co.) (See Resources)

INTEGRATION OF THE FIVE-STAGE MECHANICS

Ross, M (1987). Group process: Using therapeutic activities in chronic care. Thorofare, NJ: Slack Incorporated.

RELEVANCE OF SENSORY INTEGRATION AND OTHER THEORETICAL TREATMENT APPROACHES TO THE 5-STAGE GROUP

Abreu, BC and Toglia, JP (1987). Cognitive rehabilitation: A model for Occupational Therapy. *Am J Occup Ther* 41(7):439-448.

Abreu, BC (1985). Perceptual-cognitive rehabilitation: An occupational therapy model. Physical Disabilities SIS Newsletter, 8(1) (March).

Abreu, BC and Toglia, JP (1985). Cognitive rehabilitation. 5th ed. New York, NY: East Village Copy Center.

Adler, LJ (1983). Neurodevelopmental treatment perspective of disorders in sensory integration. Sensory Integration SIS Newsletter, 6(4).

Allen, CK (1985). Occupational therapy for psychiatric diseases: Measurement and management of cognitive disabilities. Boston, MA: Little, Brown and Co.

Allen, CK (1987). Activity: Occupational therapy's treatment method. *Am J Occup Ther* 41(9):563-575.

Allen, CK (1988). Cognitive disabilities. *Focus.* Rockville, MD: American Occupational Therapy Association Inc.

Ayres, AJ (1972). Sensory integration and learning disorders. Los Angeles, CA: Western Psychological Services.

Ayres, AJ (1979). Sensory integration and the child. Los Angeles, CA: Western Psychological Services.

Barnes, JF (1988). Myofascial Release Seminar I. Seminar presented in September at the Pain and Stress Control Center, 10 So Leopard Rd, Paoli, PA 19301.

Bobath, B and Bobath, K (1975). Motor development in the different types of Cerebral Palsy. London and Tonbridge: Whitefriars Press Ltd.

Bobath, B. The concept of "Neuro-Developmental Treatment." Notes for a presentation given at The Western Cerebral Palsy Centre, 20 Wellington Rd., London NW8, England. Date unknown.

Brown, EJ (1988). Wherever it came from, Myofascial Release works. *Advance,* 4(31) (August 8).

Corcoran, M and Barrett, D (1987). Using sensory integration principles with regressed elderly patients. New York, NY: The Haworth Press, Inc.

Davies, PM (1985). Steps to follow, a guide to the treatment of adult hemiplegia. Berlin: Springer-Verlag.

DiJoseph, L (1984). Motor behavior vs motor control: Holistic approach to movement. Sensory Integration SIS Newsletter 7(1).

Eggers, O (1987). Occupational therapy in the treatment of adult hemiplegia. Rockville, MD: Aspen Publications.

Feldenkrais, M (1979). Body & mature behavior. New York, NY: International Universities Press.

Gilfoyle, EM, Grady, AP and Moore, JC (1990). Children adapt. 2nd ed. Thorofare, NJ: Slack Inc.

Henderson, A (1988). Occupational therapy knowledge: From practice to theory. 1988 Eleanor Clarke Slagel Lecture. *Am J Occup Ther* 42(9):567-676.

Henderson, A (1988). OTs challenged to do research. *Advance,* 4(43) (October 31).

Nolen, NR (1988). Functional skill regression in late-stage dementias. *Am J Occup Ther* 42(10):666-669.

Robinson, VM (1977). Humor and the health professions. Thorofare, NJ: Slack Inc.

Ross, M (1987). Group process: Using therapeutic activities in chronic care. Thorofare, NJ: Slack Inc.

Sensory Integration International; Neurobiological Foundation for Sensory Integration (1988). Seminar presented in September at Boston University, Boston, MA.

Shell, SM (1988). Myofascial release: A total body relaxation effect. *OT Forum,* Oct 10, 1988.

Silberzahn, "Development of Sensory Integration Therapy and Practice," as cited by Scardina V: "Sensory Integration and Its Relationship to the Practice of Therapy." Seminar presented at Hartford, CT. April 1983.

Sukiennicki, DR (1979). Mobility dysfunction and its management. In Banus et al, The Developmental Therapist, 2e. Thorofare, NJ: Slack Inc.

Voss, DE (1972). Proprioceptive neuromuscular facilitation; the PNF method. In Pearson, PH and Williams, EH (Eds). Physical therapy services in developmental disabilities, pp. 223-281. Springfield, IL: Charles C. Thomas.

Weinstein, E (1988). Modern holism has ancient roots. *Advance,* 4(48) (December 12).

Hopkins and Smith (Eds) (1983). Willard and Spackman: Occupational Therapy. Philadelphia, PA: JB Lippincott Co.

CONDUCTING THE FIVE STAGE GROUP

Allen, CK (1985). Occupational therapy for psychiatric diseases: Measurement and management of cognitive disabilities. Boston, MA: Little, Brown and Co.

DLM Teaching Resources (See Resources)

Eggers, O (1987). Occupational therapy in the treatment of adult hemiplegia. Rockville, MD: Aspen Publication.

Hasselkus, BR and Kiernat, JM (1989). Nationally speaking-not by age alone: Gerontology as a specialty in occupational therapy. *Am J Occup Ther* 43(2):77-79.

Herrick, JT and Lowe, HE (1988). Can sensorimotor training help adults with mental retardation? *OT Forum III* (48). (Atlantic Edition) King of Prussia, PA.

Herrick, JT and Lowe, HE (1988). A Blueprint for habilitation programming with the adult retarded. Tape of a paper presented at the 68th Annual Conference of the American Occupational Therapy Association, Phoenix, AZ. (Also authored Adults Skills Evaluation Survey for Persons with Mental Retardation (ASES). Available from Helen E. Lowe, OTR, 130 North Fair Oaks Ave., Pasadena, CA 91103. Updated since 1984, ASES is an assessment tool designed to estimate the prevocational ability levels of adults with mild to moderate retardation in work-related settings in four domains relating to occupational role performance in fine motor skills, perceptual skills, academic skills and activities of daily living.)

Kielhofner, G and Miyake, S (1981). The therapeutic use of games with mentally retarded adults. *Am J Occup Ther* 35(6):375-382.

King, LJ. Telephone conversation with author, March 1989.

Ledermann, EF (1984). Occupational therapy in mental retardation. Springfield, IL: Charles C. Thomas.

Parachek, JF and King, LJ (1986). Parachek geriatric rating scale and treatment manual. Phoenix, AZ: Center for Neurodevelopmental Studies, Inc.

Ross, M (1987). Group process: Using therapeutic activities in chronic care. Thorofare, NJ: SLACK Incorporated.

Schon, DA (1988). Reflection in and on the practice of OT: A research perspective. Tape of a paper presented at the 68th Annual Conference of the American Occupational Therapy Association, Phoenix, AZ.

World Wide Games (See Resources).

SARIB

American Occupational Therapy Association (1988). Uniform terminology for occupational therapy. 2nd ed. Rockville, MD: The American Occupational Therapy Association.

Ayres, AJ (1972). Sensory integration and learning disorders. Los Angeles, CA: Western Psychological Services.

Clements, SD, and Peters, JE (1962). Minimal brian dysfunction in the school age child. *Archives of General Psychiatry, 6,* 185-197.

Davies, PM (1985). Steps to follow: A guide to the treatment of adult hemiplegia. New York, NY: Springer-Verlag.

Hemphill, BJ (Ed) (1982). The evaluative process in psychiatric occupational therapy. Thorofare, NJ: Slack Incorporated.

Llorens, LA (1982). Occupational therapy sequential client care record manual. Laurel, MD: Ramsco Publishing Co.

Llorens, LA and Rubin, EZ (1967). Developing ego functions in disturbed children. Detroit, MI: Wayne State University Press.

Pedretti, LW (1985). Occupational therapy practice skills for physical dysfunction. 2nd ed. St. Louis, MO: C.V. Mosby Co.

Pratt, PN and Allen, AS (1989). Occupational therapy for children. 2nd ed. St.

Louis, MO: C.V. Mosby Co.

Ross, M and Burdick, D (1981). Sensory integration: A training manual for therapists and teachers for regressed, psychiatric and geriatric patient groups. Thorofare, NJ: Slack Incorporated.

Schilder, P (1950). The image and appearance of the human body. New York, NY: International Universities Press, Inc.

Schilder, P (1951). Brain and personality. New York, NY: International Universities Press, Inc.

Schilder, P (1964). Contributions to developmental neuropsychiatry. New York NY: International Universities Press, Inc.

Siev, E, Freishtat, B and Zoltan, B (1986). Perceptual and cognitive dysfunction in the adult stroke patient: A manual for evaluation and treatment. Rev. ed. Thorofare, NJ: Slack Incorporated.

Silver, AA, and Hagin, RA (1960). Specific reading disability: delineation of the syndrome and relationship to cerebral dominance. *Comprehensive Psychiatry, 1,* 126-134.

Trombly, CA (1989). Occupational therapy for physical dysfunction. 3rd ed. Baltimore, MD: Williams & Wilkins.

RESOURCES
Computer, Robot Resources
COMPUTER OPTIONS FOR THE EXCEPTIONAL
  85 Market Street
  Poughkeepsie, NY 12601
  A complete resource for computer application in regular and special education. The catalog provides an excellent description of services and products.

COMMUNICATION AIDS FOR CHILDREN AND ADULTS, CRESTWOOD COMPANY
  P.O. Box 04606
  Milwaukee, Wisconsin 53204-0606
  Robots and switches are featured that can be put to use immediately.

LAUREATE LEARNING SYSTEMS, INC.
  110 East Spring Street
  Winooski, VT 05404
  Talking software for special education and rehabilitation.

SUNBURST COMMUNICATIONS
   101 Castleton Street
   Pleasantville, NY 10570-3498
   This company offers a variety of catalogs for a variety of needs for all age groups. They also have videocassettes and film strips. They are consumer friendly.

General Resources for Equipment, Games and Articles

CREATIVE CRAFTS INTERNATIONAL
   16 Plains Rd., Box 819
   Essex, CT 06426
   New craft concepts for education, recreation and therapy.

DLM TEACHING RESOURCES
   World Headquarters: 1 DLM Park
   Allen, Texas 75002
      Toll Free 800-527-4747 (In Texas 800-442-4711)

HEARTLAND
   P.O. Box 1151
   Sterling, IL 61081
   Aids to daily living to include evaluation apparatus, exercise and personal care.

S & S ARTS & CRAFTS
   Colchester, CT 06415
   Excellent resource for crafts and objects to use in movement.

SMITH & NEPHEW ROLYAN
   N93 W14475 Whittaker Way
   Menomonee Falls, WI 53051
   Objects to use in movement, etc.

FLAGHOUSE
   150 No. MacQuesten Pkwy
   Mt. Vernon, NY 10550
   Products for body movement and occupational therapy.

TALICOR INCORPORATED (formerly The Ungame Company)
   190 Arovista Circle
   Brea, California 92621
   Games to teach a variety of health subjects, this company produced the excellent set of leading questions used in the family communication game.

THERAPY SKILL BUILDERS
    3830 E. Bellevue, Dept. C
    Tucson, Arizona 85716
        Products for all age groups.

WESTERN PSYCHOLOGICAL SERVICES
    12031 Wilshire Blvd.
    Los Angeles, California 90025
        Publishes the "Elizur Test of Psycho-Organicity: Children and Adults"
    by Abraham Elizur, PhD

WOLVERINE SPORTS
    745 State Circle Box 1941
    Ann Arbor, Michigan 48106

WORLD WIDE GAMES
    Colchester, CT 06415

Music Resources
KIMBO EDUCATIONAL
    10 North Third Ave.
    Long Branch, New Jersey 07740

PERIPOLE
    Browns Mills, NJ 08015-0146

Index

Tongue to lip movements test, 125
Touch discrimination activities, 28
Touching, 6

Unilateral neglect test, 134

Verbalization, 33
Vestibular stimulation, 19
Vibrator
    guidelines for use of, 84-86

precautions for use of, 86-87
types of, 86
used during Stage I, 6-7
value of, 83-84
Virginia Reel, 21
Visual performance test, 120-122

Wahl Vibrators, 86
Weight estimation activities, 26
Welcoming, 5-6
Work service programs, 76